The LOVE LANGUAGES *of* GOD

The LOVE LANGUAGES *of* GOD

GARY CHAPMAN

NORTHFIELD PUBLISHING

CHICAGO

All Scripture quotations, unless otherwise indicated, are taken from the *Holy Bible, New International Version*®. NIV®. Copyright © 1973, 1978, 1984 by International Bible Society. Used by permission of Zondervan Publishing House. All rights reserved.

Scripture quotations marked NASB are taken from the *New American Standard Bible*®, © Copyright The Lockman Foundation 1960, 1962, 1963, 1968, 1971, 1972, 1973, 1975, 1977, 1995. Used by permission.

Scripture quotations marked KJV are taken from the King James Version.

Library of Congress Cataloging-in-Publication Data

Chaptman, Gary D., 1938-
    The love languages of God / Gary Chapman.
      p. cm.
    Includes bibliographical references.
    ISBN 1-881273-93-8
    ISBN 978-1-881273-93-6
      1. Love--Religious aspects--Christianity. I. Title.

BV4639 .C425 2002
241´.4--dc21   2002071862

We hope you enjoy this book from Northfield Publishing. Our goal is to provide high-quality, thought-provoking books and products that connect truth to your real needs and challenges. For more information on other books and products written and produced from a biblical perspective, go to www.moodypublishers.com or write to:

Northfield Publishing
820 N. LaSalle Boulevard
Chicago, IL 60610

7 9 10 8

Printed in the United States of America

To my sister,
Sandra Lane Benfield,
who loved God as intensely as anyone I have ever known,
and expressed it by serving others.
Though younger than I, she beat me to the finish line.
I pray that my love will be as transparent as hers.

CONTENTS

ACKNOWLEDGMENTS

*T*HIS BOOK COULD NOT HAVE BEEN written in the isolation of an ivory tower. Wherever the love of God is experienced, it is always personal, intimate, and life changing. I am indebted to the scores of people who allowed me into the inner chambers of their own encounters with God.

Without this private information, the book would have been an academic treatise. For the most part, I have used fictitious names, but the people are real, and their stories an accurate account of what they told me. To all of them, I am deeply grateful.

For technical help, I have relied again upon Tricia Kube, my secretary and administrative assistant for the past nineteen years. As always, editor Jim Vincent of Northfield Publishing has offered numerous suggestions that have enhanced the book. The editorial, production, and marketing staffs of Northfield are not only my colleagues, but my friends. My gratitude for them runs deep.

My wife, Karolyn, has for forty years been my chief cheerleader. I have often felt God's love through her words of encouragement. In the midst of writing this book, we experienced the death of my sister, my only sibling, to whom this book is dedicated, and twelve hours later, the birth of our first grandson. Through the emotions that accompany death and birth, she walked with me. Two are truly better than one.

To my sister's family—husband Reid and daughters Traci, Jill, and Allison—I can only pray that the love of God, which she experienced and freely gave, will spill over on you and me, and that we may be as faithful as she.

INTRODUCTION:
The Love Connection

SUSAN WAS MY FIRST APPOINTMENT of the day, and I felt like crying when I heard her story. Her father had committed suicide when she was thirteen. Her brother was killed in Vietnam. Six months ago, her husband left her for another woman. She and her two small children now lived with her mother. I felt like crying . . . but Susan wasn't crying. In fact, she was vibrant, almost radiant.

Assuming she was in denial of her grief, I said, "You must feel very rejected by your husband."

"I did at first, but I've come to realize that my husband is not running from me. He is running from himself. He is a very unhappy man. I think he thought that our marriage would make him happy, but you and I both know that only God can make a person truly happy."

Thinking that perhaps Susan was trying to spiritualize her pain, I said, "You have been through a lot in your life: your father's death, your brother's death, your husband's departure. How can you be so strong in your faith?"

"For one reason," she said. "I know that God loves me, so no matter what, He is always there for me."

"How can you be so sure?" I asked.

"It's a personal thing. Every morning, I give the day to God and ask Him to lead me. I read a chapter in the Bible and listen to what He says to me. God and I are very close. That's the only way I can make it."

At three o'clock that afternoon, I had an appointment with Regina. Her parents had divorced when she was ten years old. She saw her father only twice after the divorce: once at her high school graduation and again at her younger sister's funeral. Her sister had been killed in an auto accident at the age of twenty-one. Regina had been married and divorced three times; the longest of her marriages had lasted two and one-half years. She was in my office because she was contemplating a fourth marriage. Her mother had asked that she talk with me before she married again.

"I don't know if I should do this or not," Regina said. "I don't want to grow old alone, but I don't have a very good track record with marriage. I feel like I am a loser. My mother keeps telling me that God loves me and has a plan for my life. Right now I don't feel God's love, and I think I must have missed the plan. I'm not even sure there is a God."

Two ladies, each having experienced enough pain for a lifetime. One feels deeply loved by God; the other feels empty. Why do some people claim to experience God's love very deeply, while others feel so distant from God that they are unsure God even exists? I believe the answer lies in the nature of love itself. Love is not a solo experience. Love requires both a lover and a responder. If God is the divine lover, why do not all of His creatures feel His love? Perhaps because some are looking in the wrong direction.

Most often, one's search for God is influenced by culture. If our culture says, "This is the way to God," then we tend to pursue accordingly. But love is a matter of the heart, the soul, not ritual or religion. I am convinced that each of us has a "primary love language," and when we listen to God in our "heart language," we will experience His love most intimately. I am also convinced that God speaks your "love language" fluently. Perhaps this is best understood by examining how love works in human relationships.

HEARING THE LANGUAGE OF LOVE

In other volumes, I have dealt with the problem of not hearing love in our own language. My clinical research has revealed that each person has a different "love language." Thus, if parents don't speak the child's primary love language, the child will not feel loved, regardless of how sincere the parents may be. The key is learning the primary love language of each child and speaking it regularly. The same principle is true in marriage. If a husband doesn't speak his wife's love language, she won't feel loved—and her need for love goes unfulfilled.

The Five Love Languages (which has now been translated into more than twenty-five languages) focuses on helping couples learn how to effectively communicate love. Later, I teamed up with psychiatrist Ross Campbell and wrote *The Five Love Languages of Children*. This book helps parents make the same discoveries and learn how to love their children effectively. Most recently, I wrote *The Five Love Languages of Teenagers,* which is designed to help parents navigate the turbulent waters of loving their children through the adolescent years.

For those individuals who have the "will," these books can provide the "knowledge." But there are a significant number of people for whom knowledge is not enough. (Actually, all of us fall into this category from time to time.) We know what to do but don't have the "will" to do it. One husband, having heard my ideas on learning to speak your spouse's primary love language, said, "I'll tell you right now, if it's going to take my washing dishes, vacuuming floors, and doing laundry for her to feel loved, you can forget that." Obviously his problem was not "knowledge." He lacked the "will" to love his wife.

The tragedy is that people who choose not to love are never happy people. Their lack of love hurts not only the other person, but it atrophies their own souls. People who refuse to love live on the edge of desperation. I have spent a lifetime trying to help people who, to use a line from Oscar Hammerstein's *Show Boat,* are "tired of living and scared of dying." The purpose of this book is to bring people closer to God so that they can experience His limitless love and thus more effectively love others. In so doing, we help people enjoy living and have peace about dying.

TO LOVE AND TO BE LOVED

To love and to be loved—what could be more important? I believe that the key to learning and choosing love is tapping into divine love.

This is not intended to be a religious book. If a religious system was going to solve the problem of a loveless society, it would have already been solved. This book is an attempt to help people relate to "the God who is there," not the gods we have created. I have chosen not to write in the academic language of psychology or theology, but in the language of the common man, so that we can hear God's language spoken in our "heart language."

If you believe in God, and if you would like to be a lover, then this book is for you. If you don't believe in God but don't mind hanging out with people who do, I invite you on the journey. I will make every effort to respect your beliefs, while I share my own as clearly as I can.

If we are created in the image of God and are His children, we would expect Him to love us. Also, it would be natural for us to both receive love and reciprocate that love. This is illustrated in the parent–child relationship.

CONNECTING TO A PARENT'S LOVE

For parents, loving children is as natural as eating is for the child. Parents love because they are related to their children. In a very real sense, the child is a creation of the parents and bears in his/her body and spirit something of each parent's mark. It would be extremely unnatural for parents not to love their own children. I think it would be safe to say and widely agreed upon that parental love is a part of human nature. It is not something we work to attain. It is a part of who we are as human beings.

A parent's love for his or her own children (and a grand-parent's love for his or her own grandchildren) is more intense than the love he has for the child next door (or the grandchild who belongs to our best friend). But this love is not simply a genetic bonding, for adoptive parents and grandparents love their children just as intensely. There is an emotional and spiritual bonding with those children whom we consider to be "our children." We are willing to expend time, energy, and money for their well-being. We want them to learn and develop their potential. We desire that they accomplish great things in life. We are willing to give much of ourselves in order to enhance their lives. We love them. This is the normal emotional response of parents to children and grandparents to grandchildren.

The naturalness of parental love is highlighted by the reality of the few parents and grandparents who do not experience such love for children and grandchildren. The absence of parental love is so abnormal that these parents are considered dysfunctional. Everyone agrees that such parents need psychological and spiritual therapy. Loving one's children and grandchildren is as natural as loving oneself, for indeed, they are extensions of us.

REFLECTING DIVINE LOVE

I believe that parental love is a reflection of divine love. In God's eyes, we are His children, and He loves us as we love our own children. *World Book Encyclopedia* describes God as "the Supreme Being, the Creator and Ruler of the Universe, All Knowing, All Powerful, Infinite, and Ever Present."[1] Throughout man's history and across racial and cultural boundaries, millions of people have believed in the existence of such a God. The ancient Hebrew writings began with the assumption of an all-powerful God who created the heavens and the earth. Then on earth, in an orderly fashion, He created plant life and animal life and culminated His creation by making man in the image of the divine.[2]

>-<

If it is true that man is made in the image of God, then we would expect that God's love for mankind would be in a category different from God's love for the rest of His creation. We would also expect that man would be capable of responding to God's love. What research has revealed is that not only does man have the potential for responding to the love of God but, in fact, man is not fully content until he has made a love connection with God. Victor Frankl, who survived Nazi imprisonment in four concentration camps, including ones in Bohemia and at Auschwitz, reminded us that at the heart of man's existence is his search for meaning. Saint Augustine reminded us that man never truly finds ultimate meaning until he responds to the love of God.

Brian, a friend of mine, was touring Russia after the collapse of communism. He noticed that on Sunday the churches were filled with people. Knowing that for seventy years Russia had been an atheistic society and that a whole generation had been taught that God does not exist, he was intrigued to notice that so many young people were attending church. He asked his young female guide, a former member of the KGB, if people had flocked to the churches immediately when given the freedom to do so.

"No," she said. "At first, it was only the older people. Then the young people began to attend. Now all the churches are filled."

"Why do you think that is true?" Brian inquired.

"Earlier," she said, "we believed that our political leaders were gods. Now we know that is not the case. We have learned that man is man and God is God. Now we wish to know more of God."

If man is truly made in the image of God, this response is what we would expect. In spite of all governmental efforts to stamp out the belief in God, the human heart still craves the Father's love.

This father-hunger is reflected in human relationships. In his book *Life Without Father,* David Popenoe, a sociology professor at Rutgers University, gives compelling evidence that all children crave the love not only of a mother but also of a father. Something within the souls of children knows that they need his love to be secure and happy. When that love is not experienced, a child lives with an undefinable longing. Children want to love and be loved by both parents. Popenoe believes that the lack of this love connection is the major malignancy with which we enter the twenty-first century.

REESTABLISHING
THE LOVE CONNECTION

Similarly, we need to reestablish the love connection with God. To know God and to love God should be our chief end; all else is simply background music. When we learn to know and love Him, we will have made the "love connection."

What I hope to do in the remaining chapters of this book is to share with the reader what I have learned about love in over thirty years of marriage and family counseling. I believe that human love relationships reflect the nature of God, who is love. If we can understand the dynamics of human love, it will help us understand the expressions of divine love.

I want to do this by introducing you to friends I have met along my own journey. (In most instances, only first names have been used [and changed] and details altered to protect privacy.) Some I have known for many years; others are more recent acquaintances, but all of them have made the "love connection" with God.

1

⚬⚬⚬

UNDERSTANDING THE FIVE LOVE LANGUAGES

*B*EFORE I TAKE YOU ON A JOURNEY into the lives of my friends, let me first share with you the basic paradigm that has helped many individuals make love connections on the human level. After more than thirty years of counseling couples and families, I am convinced that there are only five basic languages of love. There are many dialects but only five basic languages.

Each of us has a primary love language. That is, one of the five love languages speaks more deeply to us emotionally than the other four. When someone speaks my primary love language, I am drawn to that person because he or she is meeting my basic need to feel loved. When a person does not speak my primary language, I will wonder whether he or she really loves me, because emotionally I am not understanding that person.

The problem in many human relationships is that you and I speak our own love language and wonder why the other person does not understand. That's like my speaking English to someone who only understands German and wondering why he doesn't comprehend my message. Human relationships are greatly enhanced when we learn to speak the other person's love language.

It works. Thousands of married couples echo the story of Scott and Anna. They had driven four hundred miles to Atlanta to attend a "Love Languages" seminar. After the Friday night session, Scott said, "Dr. Chapman, we want to thank you for turning our marriage around."

I couldn't figure it out. They had just started the weekend seminar.

Sensing the question in my eyes, he continued. "I know that you don't know us, but God used the love language concept to transform our marriage. We have been married for thirty-three years, but to be very honest with you, the last twenty years have been utterly miserable. We have lived in the same house and been outwardly friendly with each other, but that's as far as it went. If you want to know how bad it was, we had not taken a vacation together in twenty years. We simply didn't like being with each other.

"Some time ago, I shared my misery with a friend. He went into his house and came back with your book and told me to read it. He thought it would help me. I went home and read it. I finished reading it about two o'clock one morning. I shook my head and asked myself, *How could I have missed this?*

"I realized immediately that my wife and I had not spoken each other's love language for years. I gave the book to her and asked her to read it and let me know what she thought of it. Three or four days later, we sat down and discussed the book. We both agreed that if we had read the book twenty years earlier, our lives would have been different. I asked her if she thought it would make any difference if we tried now. She replied, 'We don't have anything to lose.'"

LANGUAGES THAT TRANSFORM

At this point, Anna broke into the conversation and said, "I didn't have any idea that things would actually change between us, but I was certainly willing to give it a try. I still can't believe what has happened. We enjoy being with each other now. Two months ago, we took our first vacation together and had a wonderful time."

During the conversation, I learned that Scott's love language was words of affirmation and Anna's love language was gifts. Scott was not a gift-giver by nature. In fact, gifts meant very little to him. He got no special thrill when he received a gift, and he had little interest in giving gifts. Conversely, Anna was a woman of few words. She was not given to compliments and admitted that she was often critical.

It was not without effort that Scott learned to buy gifts. In fact, he recruited his sister to help him with the project. Anna admitted that at first she thought it would be a temporary phenomenon. Their original agreement was that for three months they would speak each other's love language at least once a week and see what happened. "Within two months," Scott said, "I had warm feelings for Anna and she had feelings for me." Anna said, "I never dreamed that I would be able to say the words 'I love you' to Scott and really mean it. But I do; it's incredible how much I love him."

When a married couple discover each other's primary

love language and choose to speak it on a regular basis, emotional love will be reborn.

Single adults have also benefited greatly from understanding the five love languages. Megan wrote me from Japan.

Dear Dr. Chapman,

I wanted to write you and let you know how much your book, *The Five Love Languages,* has meant to me. I know you wrote it for married couples but a friend of mine gave it to me and it has had a profound impact on my life. I am in Japan teaching English as a second language. The main reason I came here was to get away from my mother. Our relationship has been strained for several years. I felt unloved and that she was trying to control my life. When I read your book, my eyes were opened. I realized that my love language is words of affirmation, but my mother only gave me critical, harsh words.

I also realized that my mother's language was acts of service. She was forever doing something for me. Even after I got my own apartment, she wanted to come over and vacuum my floors. She knitted a sweater for my dachshund and baked cookies when she knew I was having friends over. Since I didn't feel loved by her, I saw all of these as efforts to control my life. Now I realize it was her way of expressing love to me. She was speaking her love language and I know now that she was sincere.

I mailed a copy of the book to her. She read it, and we discussed it via E-mail. I apologized for misreading her actions over the years. And after I explained to her how deeply her critical words had hurt me, she apologized to me. Now her E-mails are filled with words of affirmation. And I find myself thinking about things I can do for her when I get home. I have already told her that I want to paint the bedroom for her. She can't do it herself and can't afford to have it done.

I know that our relationship is going to be different. I have helped some students here learn to speak English a little better, but my greatest discovery has been the languages of love.

LANGUAGES THAT TRANSFORM CHILDREN AND TEENS

Parents also must learn the primary love languages of their children if the children are to feel loved. Thirty-three-year-old Marta was the mother of two young children, ages five and a half and six months. About two months after the baby came, Marta began to notice a change in Brent. Prior to the second child, he had been "a perfect child," she said. "We never had any trouble with him. But almost overnight we began to see behaviors that we had not seen before."

Transforming Brent

"He would do things that he knew were against the rules and then deny that he had done them. We noticed that he was deliberately rough in handling the baby; once I found him pulling the blanket over the baby's head in the crib. He began to defy me. I remember the time he said, 'No, and you can't make me.'"

About the time of Brent's defiant statement, Marta began attending a ladies' study group that was studying *The Five Love Languages of Children*. "When I read the chapter on quality time, I knew what was going on with Brent," Marta said. "I had never thought of it before, but I knew that quality time was Brent's primary love language. Before the baby came, I spoke his language loudly and he felt loved. After the baby came, we no longer took walks in the park together, and our quality time was greatly diminished. With this insight, I went home determined to make time for Brent. Rather than doing housework while the baby slept, I determined to give him quality time.

"It was amazing to watch the results. Within four or five days, Brent was back to being the happy child he had always been. I couldn't believe how quickly he had changed."

The craving for love is our deepest emotional need whether we are children or adults. If we feel loved by the significant people in our lives, the world looks bright, and we are free to develop our interests and make a positive contribution in the world. But if our love tank is empty and we do not feel loved by the significant people in our lives, then the world begins to look dark and this darkness will be reflected in our behavior.

Transforming Our Teens

Much of the violence among teenagers in our society is rooted in their having empty love tanks. In the heart of the teenager, love has to do with *connection, acceptance,* and *nurture.* Connection requires the physical presence of the parent and meaningful communication. Acceptance implies unconditional love regardless of the behavior of the teen, while nurture is feeding the spirit of the teen with encouragement and comfort. The opposite of connection is abandonment. The opposite of acceptance is rejection, and the opposite of nurture is abuse—physical or verbal.

The teen who feels abandoned, rejected, or abused will

almost certainly struggle with self-worth, meaning, and purpose. His or her love tank will be empty, and eventually the pain of feeling unloved will show up in the destructive behavior of the teenager.

Negative behavior often changes radically and quickly when the teenager genuinely feels loved by parents. Speaking our teens' love languages can transform our relationships with them.

THE FIVE LOVE LANGUAGES

Let me briefly describe the five love languages for those who have not read my previous books.

1. Words of Affirmation

Using words to affirm the other person is a key way to express love. "You look nice in that dress. . . . You did a good job with that assignment. . . . I appreciate your sticking with this until you finished. . . . Thanks for cleaning your room. . . . I appreciate you taking out the garbage." These are all affirming words. Here are others: "I know you worked hard on this project and I want you to know that I sincerely appreciate what you have done. . . . This was a great meal. . . . Thanks for all your hard work."

There are thousands of ways to express affirmation by words. These affirmations may focus upon the person's behavior, physical appearance, or personality. The words may be spoken, written, or even sung. To the people whose primary love language is words of affirmation, such affirming words fall like a spring rain on barren soil.

2. Quality Time

Quality time is giving someone your undivided attention. With a small child, it is sitting on the floor rolling the ball back and forth. With a spouse, it is sitting on the couch, looking at each other and talking, or taking a walk down the road, just the two of you, or going out to eat together and looking and talking to each other. It is taking a teenager fishing and telling him what life was like when you were a teenager, then asking how his life differs from yours. You are focusing on the teen—not the fishing.

For the single adult, quality time is planning an event with a friend where the two of you can have some time to share your life with each other. The important thing is not the activity but that the two of you have time together. When you give someone quality time, you are giving him or her a part of your life. It is a deep communication of love.

3. Gifts

Giving gifts is a universal expression of love. Gifts say, "He was thinking about me. Look what he got for me." Children, adults, and teenagers all appreciate gifts. For some people, gifts is their primary love language. Nothing makes them feel more loved than receiving a gift.

Gifts need not be expensive. You can pick up a colored, twisted stone while hiking, take it home, and give it to a ten-year-old boy, tell him where you found it, and tell him you were thinking of him. I can almost guarantee you when he is twenty-three, he will still have the stone in his dresser drawer.

4. Acts of Service

"Actions speak louder than words," the old saying goes. That's true for people whose primary love language is acts of service. Doing something that you know the other person would like for you to do is an expression of love. So is cooking a meal, washing dishes, vacuuming floors, mowing grass, cleaning the grill, giving the dog a bath, painting a bedroom, washing the car, driving the sixth grader to soccer practice, mending a doll dress, and putting the chain back on a bicycle. The list could be endless. The person who speaks this language is always looking for things he can do for others.

To the person whose primary love language is acts of service, words may indeed be empty if they are not accompanied by acts of service. The husband says, "I love you," and she's thinking, *If he loved me, he would do something around here.* He may be sincere in his words of affirmation, but he is missing her emotionally because her language is acts of service; without it, she does not feel loved.

A wife gives her husband gifts, but if his love language is acts of service, he is wondering, *Why doesn't she spend her time cleaning the house instead of buying me gifts?* "The way to a man's heart is through his stomach" is not true for all men but may well be true for the man whose primary love language is acts of service.

5. Physical Touch

We have long known the emotional power of physical touch. That's why we pick up babies, hold them, cuddle them, and say all those silly words. And long before the child understands the meaning of love, the child feels loved by physical touch. Hugging and kissing a six-year-old as he or she leaves for school in the morning is a way of filling the child's love tank and thus preparing him for a day of learning.

If the child's primary love language is physical touch, nothing is more important. The teenager whose primary love language is physical touch may draw back from your hugs and kisses, but it does not mean that he has no desire for touch. He associates hugs and kisses with childhood. He is not a child any longer. So you must learn new dialects, new ways of touching the teenager. A slap on the shoulder, an elbow at an appropriate moment, wrestling the teenager to the floor, a back rub after a tough football practice will fill the teenager's love tank. Stop touching this teenager, and he or she will feel unloved.

THE GOAL: A FULL LOVE TANK

The key to making sure that your spouse, your children, your parents feel loved is to discover the primary love language of the other person and speak it consistently. If you speak her primary love language, her love tank will be full and she will be secure in your love. Then you can sprinkle in the other four and these will be "icing on the cake." However, if you don't speak a person's primary love language, she (or he) will not feel loved even though you may be speaking some of the other languages.

WHAT LOVE LANGUAGE
DOES GOD SPEAK?

Now let's return to the theme of this book: the love languages of God. It is my premise that the love languages observed in human relationships are a reflection of divine love. If man is indeed made in the image of God, then we would expect to find all five love languages expressed in the character and nature of God. It is also my premise that God speaks all five love languages fluently and that people tend to be attracted to God most deeply when they sense that God is speaking their primary love language.

I believe these premises can be proven from both the self-revelation of God found in the Holy Scriptures and from human experience. In the pages that follow, we will enter the private lives of contemporary and historical individuals who have claimed to have a love relationship with God. We will examine the nature of these relationships. In so doing, we can learn how to enhance our own love connection with God.

2

><

GOD SPEAKS
LOVE LANGUAGE #1:
Words of Affirmation

I ARRIVED AT THE CHURCH LATE. The music
was over; the sermon had begun. Pastor Reuben was wax-
ing eloquent, and his multicultural congregation was giving
him plenty of encouragement.

"That's right, Brother Reuben. Preach it!" I heard one elderly gentleman shout.

"Thank You, Jesus," a lady to my right said with her eyes
closed and her right hand lifted high.

We had driven two hours from Chicago's O'Hare Airport
through heavy snow to reach this inner-city church. I had tak-
en a seat near the back of the church, where I tried to be in-
conspicuous. My driver, whom I had met at the airport, filled
me in on the history of the church.

"When Pastor Reuben came here," he said, "we only had

about thirty members. Now we have 2,000. The church was dead but he loved us. He knows how to motivate people, and God has blessed."

He told me about the church's ministry to the homeless—how they had turned an old warehouse three blocks from the church into a shelter. That shelter now housed more than 150 people every night. He told me about their soup kitchen. "I go down three days a week and help serve lunch," he said. "It's the highlight of my week." He told me about their recovery program for young people who were addicted to drugs.

A MESSAGE ON LOVE

I was thinking about all of this as I sat in the back of the church and listened to Pastor Reuben. He wove words together in a fascinating way. I still remember the three points of his sermon: 1. God knows you. 2. God loves you. 3. God wants you. I listened as he walked through the Old and New Testaments giving illustrations for each of his points. He talked about the Hebrew prophets as though they were his friends. He quoted Scriptures freely.

"Listen to the words of God to ancient Israel," he said. "'I have loved you with an everlasting love; therefore I have drawn you with lovingkindness.'[1] Do you think that God loved Israel more than He loves you? Listen to these words about Jesus as He faced death. 'Jesus knowing that His hour had come that He would depart out of this world to the Father, having loved His own who were in the world, He loved them to the end.'"[2]

"God has always loved his children. God will always love His children, and He wants you to be His child," Reuben said with deep passion.

><

I was tired; I was sleepy. The building was hot, but I never once nodded as I listened to this master wordsmith make his case for the love of God and called his listeners to "repentance and faith in Christ." As he gave his plea for sinners to come to Christ, several people left their seats, walked to the front, and bowed at the altar, many of them weeping. "Come home, come home," Reuben pleaded. "God loves you too and wants you to be His child."

AFTER THE MESSAGE

Eventually, the service was concluded and Reuben called me to the front and introduced me to the congregation. I had been invited to speak the next night at a marriage enrichment event for the couples of the church. Then, after the service, Reuben's wife Patsy invited me to their house for dessert along with the couple who directed their marriage enrichment ministry.

After we got acquainted and were beginning to relax, I said to Patsy, "Describe your husband to me. What kind of man is he?" (Being a marriage counselor, you can get away with these kinds of questions.) "Oh, he is definitely a romantic," she said. "He writes me poems; sometimes he sings songs to me. He gives me speeches about how wonderful I am."

"Then you must have a full love tank," I said.

"That's the problem. I've read your book, and my love language is acts of service. I want him to wash the dishes," she said, laughing. "You know, vacuum the floor, take out the garbage, help me around the house. I know he loves me, but sometimes I don't feel loved. His words sometimes seem empty. It's almost like he's trying to humor me. I know he's sincere, but I need more than words."

I sensed that this conversation had gone a little deeper than I or Reuben had intended, so I said to Patsy, "You sound like my wife. Her love language is also acts of service. It took me a long time to get the connection between washing dishes and love." I laughed and changed the subject. Reuben was also laughing, and in less than a minute we were talking about the Chicago Bears.

The next night after the marriage enrichment session was over, Reuben drove me to my hotel after dropping Patsy off at their house. As we drove away from the house, Reuben said, "You have stimulated my thinking. I've got a good wife. We've been married for seventeen years, but I'm not sure that I'm meeting her emotional needs. This love language concept has opened my eyes. I'm definitely going to read your book. I think I've got some homework to do."

I was impressed by Reuben's sensitivity and openness. I shared more about my own marriage and how long it took me to discover the love language of my wife. I also shared what a difference it had made in my own marriage.

A little over a year later, I met Reuben again at a national pastor's conference in Chicago. He ran up to me, gave me a big bear hug, and said, "I just want to tell you what a difference you made in my marriage and in my ministry. I have been using your five love languages in my counseling and teaching ever since you came to our church. And Patsy told me that if I saw you to tell you that I am now washing the dishes." We both had a good laugh, and I asked him if we could spend some time together that afternoon. I wanted to spend more time with this man who had made such a strong impact on so many lives.

HOW ONE PASTOR BECAME A PASTOR

Among other things that afternoon, I asked Reuben to tell me about his conversion to Christ. "Well, it's a long story," he said. "When I was a young boy, my mother took me to church. The pastor was an older man who preached often about the love of God. I remember he said, 'God will love you when everyone else walks away from you.' He talked about how God valued the individual. I remember he would say, 'Everybody is somebody in God's eyes.' He motivated me to want to be somebody. My mother always wanted me to go to college. Between her and the preacher, I decided to work hard in high school so I could get into college.

"Unfortunately, when I got to college, I got with the wrong crowd, and before long I was partying more than I was studying. One night near the end of my freshman year, I was at a drinking party and had too much to drink. The next morning, I woke up lying in a field nearby and had no idea how I'd gotten there. I sat up, wiped my eyes, and heard the birds singing. And as clear as a bell, I heard the words of my old pastor: 'God will love you when everyone else walks away from you. Everybody is somebody in God's eyes.'

"I started weeping. I knew those words were true, and I knew I was walking in the wrong direction. I wept for a long time before I said anything, and then I said to God: 'Forgive me for acting like a nobody when in Your eyes, I'm somebody. Forgive me for walking away from Your love. If You will forgive me and come into my life, I will be somebody for You.'

"It was like the scales fell off my eyes," Reuben continued. "I felt like I had come home from a long journey. I knew that God had forgiven me, and I knew that He wanted me to tell others about His love. I was saved and called to preach sitting in that field that morning.

"That weekend, I went home and told my mother what had happened. She shouted all over the house, praising God that He had saved her boy. She called the pastor and told him what had happened, and he invited me to tell the people at the church the next Sunday. So the next Sunday, I gave a testimony of what God had done in my life and that I intended to follow Him and be a preacher. And I've been walking with Him ever since. I changed my college major to speech with a minor in English. While I was a student, I preached every time I got an opportunity. When I got to seminary, a little church called me to be their pastor. So I pastored while I attended seminary."

"Do you enjoy preaching?" I asked.

"I'd rather preach than eat, and you know how preachers like to eat," he said with a smile on his face. "When I'm preaching, I feel like I'm doing what I was created to do. It's my way of saying thank You to God for what He's done for me. I feel closest to God when I'm preaching."

WORDS OF AFFIRMATION

What Reuben shared with me that afternoon stimulated the research that has led to this book. Obviously, Reuben's primary love language was words of affirmation. He spoke them freely to his wife, and I later learned that his encouraging words characterized his relationships with others. In his marriage, he had not always felt loved by Patsy because often she gave him critical words about not helping her around the house. When they learned each other's primary love language, Patsy started giving him affirming words, and he began to speak her love language—acts of service. The emotional climate of their marriage greatly improved.

What is true with our relationships on the human level is also true in our relationship with God. What God used to get through to a wandering college freshman were words of affirmation. Reuben remembered the words of his pastor: "God will love you when everyone else walks away from you. Everybody is somebody in God's eyes." They were to his heart words from God. They moved him deeply. He knew in his heart that God loved him and that God wanted a relationship with him. Once he had "come home to God," his first desire was to express his love to God. For him, that was best done by words of affirmation. He would affirm the love of God to others through the power of the spoken word.

Some people—even some pastors—find public speaking very difficult. But not Reuben; that was his primary love language. That is why he felt closest to God when preaching. That is why preaching was his way of saying thank You to God.

Reuben knew that there were other ways to express one's love to God. He taught his congregation that when we give gifts to God (such as tithes, offerings, and our time and skills in service), we are saying "I love You," and that we also show our love to God by serving others. He emphasized the discipline of meditation and prayer in which one spends quality time with God. He also taught that we touch God by touching others. But for him, the most natural expression of his love to God was in using words both to affirm God and to encourage others.

Was Reuben's experience with God unique? Not at all. The Bible is filled with illustrations of God speaking the love language called words of affirmation. In fact, the Bible itself is often known as the "Word of God." The Old Testament prophetic books often begin with such words as these: "The word of the LORD came to Isaiah saying . . ." This phrase, "The word of the LORD came," is repeated often in the Book of Jeremiah. The New Testament puts it this way: "All Scripture is God-breathed and is useful for teaching, rebuking, correcting and training in righteousness, so that the man of God may be thoroughly equipped for every good work." Again, "You must understand that no prophecy of Scripture came about by the prophet's own interpretation. For prophecy never had its origin in the will of man, but men spoke from God as they were carried along by the Holy Spirit."[3]

THE WORD OF GOD
AND THE WORTH OF MAN

In the Beginning . . .

All of the words from God affirm man's worth. Modern nihilistic thinking concludes that man is worthless and his life has no meaning. That is not the message of the Scriptures. In the first chapter of the Bible we read, "Then God said, 'Let us make man in our image, in our likeness, and let them rule over the fish of the sea and the birds of the air, over the livestock, over all the earth, and over all the creatures that move along the ground.' So God created man in his own image, in the image of God he created him; male and female he created them."[4] Whatever else this means, it places man above the animals and gives him the capacity to have a relationship with God.

The New Testament affirms man's worth. The writer of Hebrews said (quoting the psalmist) that God made man "a little lower than the angels" and has "crowned him with glory and honor."[5]

>─<

Directing Man Toward His Highest End

All of the specific commands of God in both the Old and New Testaments affirm man's worth and flow from the love of God and direct man toward his highest end. Some people rebel against the commands of God and find them restrictive, but this is not the perspective of those who know God. They believe that the prohibitions of God are designed to keep us from those things that would destroy us. They also believe the admonitions of God are designed to help us experience life's highest good. They accept the words of the prophet Isaiah, "This is what the LORD says—your Redeemer, the Holy One of Israel:'I am the LORD your God, who teaches you what is best for you, who directs you in the way you should go. If only you had paid attention to my commands, your peace would have been like a river, your righteousness like the waves of the sea."6

The God of the Bible is characterized as the God who speaks. All of God's words affirm man's worth and are designed to build a relationship with man.

God's Encouraging Words

Read the Scriptures and hear God's words of encouragement to man:

- *"Do not fear, for I am with You; do not be dismayed, for I am your God. I will strengthen you and help you; I will uphold you with my righteous right hand."*
- *"For I know the plans I have for you . . . plans to prosper you and not to harm you, plans to give you hope and a future."*

- *"I have loved you with an everlasting love; I have drawn you with loving-kindness."*
- *"I will turn their mourning into gladness; I will give them comfort and joy instead of sorrow."*[7]

Jesus' Encouraging Words

The words of Jesus of Nazareth show His role in affirming God and bringing life and hope to all who would respond:

- *"I tell you the truth, whoever hears my word and believes him who sent me has eternal life and will not be condemned; he has crossed over from death to life."*
- *"I am the bread of life. He who comes to me will never go hungry, and he who believes in me will never be thirsty."*
- *"For my Father's will is that everyone who looks to the Son and believes in him shall have eternal life, and I will raise him up at the last day."*
- *"My sheep listen to my voice; I know them, and they follow me. I give them eternal life, and they shall never perish; no one can snatch them out of my hand. My Father, who has given them to me, is greater than all; no one can snatch them out of my Father's hand. I and the Father are one."*
- *"'Behold, I am coming soon! My reward is with me, and I will give to everyone according to what he has done. I am the Alpha and Omega, the First and the Last, the Beginning and the End. . . .' Whoever is thirsty, let him come; and whoever wishes, let him take the free gift of the water of life."*[8]

Jesus came to show the love of God, giving Himself as a sacrifice for the misdeeds of every man and woman. Jesus said He was God's Son. Who can fathom the depths of the love of Jesus, who, while being crucified, prayed, "Father, forgive them, for they do not know what they are doing."[9] The words of Jesus clearly affirmed His love for humanity. His love was unconditional.

He stated His purpose clearly when He said, "I am the gate; whoever enters through me shall be saved. . . . The thief comes only to steal and kill and destroy; I have come that they may have life, and have it to the full. I am the good shepherd. The good shepherd lays down his life for his sheep."[10]

God speaks fluently the love language words of affirmation. From beginning to end, the Bible pictures a loving God who declares His love by speaking words of truth, comfort, and redemption.

RESPONDING WITH
WORDS OF AFFIRMATION

Martin Luther: *Words for His Wife and God*

Many individuals testify that their "God connection" was stimulated by reading the Bible. Martin Luther, the young monk who sought to find peace with God by living a life of strictest asceticism, is an example. Sitting alone in his room, deeply concerned about his relationship with God, Luther opened his Bible and began to read Paul's letter to the Romans. When he came to Romans chapter 1, verse 17, he read, "The just shall live by faith" (KJV). He paused. He pondered. Then joy unspeakable flooded his heart.

Before this, he had tried hard to please God by a life of discipline. Now his eyes were opened—he understood salvation was by faith, not works. This word from God was to him the "gate to Paradise." From that moment, Martin Luther's life focused on listening to the words of God. For him, the Bible was the Word of God. That is why he moved against the established church of his day, which placed more emphasis on tradition and man's religious efforts than on the Scriptures. Martin Luther's plea was that men would return to the Word of God.

Martin Luther's primary love language seems to have been words of affirmation. Read the accounts of his life and, on the human level, you find him affirming his beautiful wife Katharine. In a letter written February 27, 1532, he began, "To my dearly beloved wife Katharine Luther, for her own hands. God greet thee in Christ, my dearly loved Katie! I hope . . . that I can come [home] tomorrow, or the day after. Pray God that he bring me home safe and sound." To Hans, his six-year-old son he wrote, "Grace and peace in Christ, my dear little son. I hear with great pleasure that you are learning your lessons so well and praying so diligently. Continue to do so, my son, and cease not."[11]

In the realm of the spiritual, Martin Luther used words to express his devotion to God. His Ninety-five Theses, carefully thought out and written down and nailed on the door of the castle church in Wittenberg, Germany, were a listing of fundamental beliefs that would light the fires of the Reformation. He used powerful words—both convicting and affirming —as he wrote numerous hymns and Bible commentaries, developed a catechism, translated the Bible from Latin to German, and delivered thousands of sermons. Words were his way of expressing his devotion to God. While other monks meditated, Luther was speaking and writing. His best-known hymn, "A Mighty Fortress Is Our God," focuses on the power of the Word of God. In verse 3, Luther wrote these words:

And tho this world, with devils filled,
Should threaten to undo us,
We will not fear, for God hath willed
His truth to triumph thru us:
The prince of darkness grim,
We tremble not for him;
His rage we can endure,
For lo, his doom is sure,
One little word shall fell him.

King David: *Giving Words of Praise*

Perhaps the best biblical example of a man whose primary love language was words of affirmation is David, the second king of Israel. On numerous occasions, David indicated how deeply he was moved by the words of God.

How sweet are your words to my taste, sweeter than honey to my mouth! I gain understanding from your precepts; therefore, I hate every wrong path. Your word is a lamp to my feet and a light for my path.

Your statutes are my heritage forever; they are the joy of my heart.

I have put my hope in your word.

I rejoice in your promise like one who finds great spoil. I hate and abhor falsehood but I love your law. Seven times a day I praise you for your righteous laws. Great peace have they who love your law, and nothing can make them stumble.[12]

In response to God's love, David used words of affirmation to express his love for God.

May those who love your salvation always say, "The LORD be exalted!"

I will praise God's name in song and glorify him with thanksgiving. This will please the LORD more than an ox, more than a bull with its horns and hoofs.

Oh, how I love your law! I meditate on it all day long. Your commands make me wiser than my enemies.

My mouth will speak in praise of the LORD. Let every creature praise his holy name for ever and ever.

Praise the LORD. Praise the LORD, O my soul. I will praise the LORD all my life; I will sing praise to my God as long as I live. [13]

Clearly David's primary vehicle of expressing his love to God was words of praise, thanksgiving, and adoration. If you have any question about David's primary love language, read Psalm 18, in which David responds to God's deliverance from his enemies. For fifty verses, he expresses his love to God in some of the most beautiful language ever written. David had only the five books of the Hebrew Bible, typically referred to as the Pentateuch or the Torah, but clearly, he saw them as the words of God.

David said of the Scriptures, "Your word, O LORD, is eternal; it stands firm in the heavens. . . . Your laws endure to this day, for all things serve you. If your law had not been my delight, I would have perished in my affliction. I will never forget your precepts, for by them you have preserved my life."[14]

David saw all of God's words—laws, ordinances, commandments, precepts, testimonies, statutes, and judgments—as being expressions of who God is. He took them as ultimate truth, as certain as God Himself. He based his life on the words of God. As best we can determine, David wrote seventy-three of the Psalms found in the Bible. Many of them are expressions of praise and thanksgiving to God. His words are some of the most emotional literature in the Bible. David clearly expressed his devotion to God through words of affirmation.

FEELING CLOSE TO GOD

For my pastor friend Reuben, for Martin Luther, and for King David, God expressed His love in words, and their primary love response to God was expressed in words. This was also true of Jason, whom I met in Riverside, California, who said to me, "My love language is words of affirmation. Once my wife started speaking affirming words, my love for her grew more intense."

Much later in our conversation, I said to my young friend, "When do you feel closest to God?"

Jason responded, "I feel closest to God when I am singing praise to Him and when I am praying. My prayers flow with praise and thanksgiving to God, telling Him how much I love Him."

Thousands of contemporary followers of Jesus can identify with Jason. Their hearts have been captured by the words of God, and they reciprocate His love by expressing words of praise.

But words of affirmation is not God's only love language,

and many contemporary Christians would have a different answer than the one Jason gave. Their method of worshiping and expressing their love to God does not focus on words but on quality time, and that brings us to the second love language of God.

3

><

GOD SPEAKS
LOVE LANGUAGE #2:
Quality Time

*A*FTER I HAD FINISHED MY LECTURE in which
I described the five love languages and the importance of
understanding and speaking each other's primary love language, Greta rushed over to me. Pointing her finger in my
face, she said excitedly, "We have got to talk." Greta had spoken earlier—we were both speakers at a national women's
conference in Los Angeles. I didn't know what she wanted
to talk about but, having heard her lecture and observed her
exuberant spirit, I was certain the conversation would not
be boring. We agreed to meet the next afternoon during the
conference "free time."

When we got together, Greta dove right into the subject. "Let me tell you my thoughts from last night. I am so
excited about this! You know that my lecture was on the

woman and her spirituality. Well, after hearing your lecture, it just struck me that God speaks to us in our primary love language. That is why some people have dramatic, emotionally moving conversions.

"For example," she continued, "my husband was converted at a church which he attended with a work colleague. The second Sunday he attended, the friend asked if he would like to go to the front of the church and have people pray for him. Not wanting to offend his friend, he agreed. Several men gathered around him and began to pray aloud all at the same time. My husband said that he had never heard anything like it. But within five minutes, my husband was weeping uncontrollably and asking God to forgive him. He said it was like God actually touched him. It was like electricity running through his body, and he felt totally clean.

"He came home and told me about it, and I didn't want to have anything to do with it. To me it was religious emotionalism, and I couldn't believe that he had gotten caught up in that. He continued to attend the church and began to bring home books for me to read.

"My own conversion was very different from my husband's. For me, it came through months of contemplation, prayer, and reading the Scriptures. I knew this spiritual experience was important to my husband, and I wanted to find out about it. That was my first motivation. But as I began to read the Scriptures, it was like God began to speak to me. I realized that what I was reading was truth and that behind the truth was a God who loved me. I never had a dramatic experience like my husband, but little by little, I began to realize that I was becoming a follower of Jesus."

Nine months after her husband's conversion, Greta was having her normal Bible reading and meditation time one morning. She came upon Revelation 3:20, where Jesus said, "Here I am! I stand at the door and knock. If anyone hears my voice and opens the door, I will come in and eat with him, and he with me." As Greta put it, "It seemed so clear that for the past several months God had been knocking at the door of my life. That morning I actually said to Him, 'Come in. I want to share the rest of my life with You.'

"I didn't cry. I wasn't emotionally excited," Greta explained. "It was a quiet, calm moment in which my heart opened up and allowed God to come into my life."

WHAT GRETA LEARNED

"Now I see it all so clearly. God spoke my husband's primary love language, physical touch, and my primary love language, quality time, and led both of us to understand He loved us," Greta said. "I have never fully understood his experience, and he wonders how I can be so calm about my relationship with God. But both of us know that we are followers of Jesus. It has had the most profound effect upon both of our lives."

Almost without taking a breath, Greta said, "Now let me tell you what else I thought about last night." (I could tell that Greta had had a busy night, but I was eager to hear.) "I realized that not only does God speak our primary love language to show His love to us, but we speak our primary love language in showing our love to God. My husband expresses his love to God by singing praise songs in church. He will lift both hands toward God, often close his eyes, and sing with all his heart. I will sometimes see tears running from his eyes as he sings. His emotions are stirred. He often says, 'I felt the presence of God.' I would never do that," said Greta. "That's just not me."

"So how do you express your love to God?" I asked.

"By spending quality time with God, of course," she said. "You didn't need to ask me that; you already knew," she said with a smile. "My greatest joy is spending time with God in studying the Scriptures. I can spend a whole morning. I lose track of time. Nothing is more important to me than my time with God. On the other hand, my husband finds it hard to spend more than ten minutes reading the Bible or a devotional book. He would much rather be in church singing praise songs and 'feeling the presence of God.' I realize now that he is as sincere as I. It's just that we speak different love languages to God."

WHAT ROD LEARNED

When I finished my conversation with Greta, I knew that she had fleshed out for me the thesis for a book I would some-day write on the love languages of God. I met Greta two years later at a marriage conference. She introduced me to her husband, Rod. "This is the man who taught me how to love you," she said to her husband. Rod had that bewildered look on his face until she said, "He wrote the book *The Five Love Languages.*"

Now Rod smiled. "Our marriage is changed," he said. "I couldn't believe it when Greta came home and started speaking my language. You will be pleased to know that we have a date night every week and every evening we have fifteen min-utes of 'couple time.' I'm making sure that Greta's love tank is full."

When I inquired about how the love language concept had affected their worship of God, Rod said, "Oh, I'm still raising my hands in praise to God and Greta is still spending her time meditating." They both laughed and Greta said, "It's true. But now we are giving each other freedom to express our love to God differently."

QUALITY TIME WITH GOD
THROUGH THE YEARS

With the Jewish Patriarchs and Ancient Israel

Biblical and postbiblical history reveals numerous illustrations of what Greta and Rod learned about experiencing the love of God. The Old Testament Scriptures picture God as spending quality time with Adam and Eve. In the cool of the evening, they walked and talked together in the Garden of Eden. It was only after the Fall that Adam and Eve hid themselves from God, knowing they had violated His love.[1]

Later, Abraham is called the "friend of God." It appears that God often spoke personally with Abraham. On one occasion when God was about to bring judgment on a wicked city in which Abraham's nephew Lot lived, God said, "Shall I hide from Abraham what I am about to do?"[2] In fact, God did not hide this information from Abraham but actually engaged in a dialogue in which Abraham sought to persuade God not to destroy the righteous along with the wicked. Bottom line, God agreed not to destroy the city if as many as ten righteous people could be found living in the city. When God brought judgment, He did deliver Abraham's nephew Lot by taking him out of the city before judgment fell.

The Psalms often speak of God's love for His creatures and His desire to draw near and spend quality time with them. For example, "The LORD is righteous in all his ways and loving toward all he has made. The LORD is near to all who call on him, to all who call on him in truth."[3] Through the prophet Isaiah, God spoke of His love for Israel and promised His presence would be with them in time of trouble. "Fear not, for I have redeemed you; I have summoned you by name; you are mine. When you pass through the waters, I will be with you; and when you pass through the rivers, they will not sweep over you."[4]

The psalmist spoke of an intimate love relationship with God based on God's willingness to give him focused attention: "I love the LORD, for he heard my voice; he heard my cry for mercy. Because he turned his ear to me, I will call on him as long as I live."[5] The psalmist was drawn to God because of God's willingness to talk with him in his time of need. The New Testament apostle James spoke of a similar relationship with God when he said, "Come near to God and he will come near to you."[6]

In the Christian Faith

The idea that the eternal God desires to spend quality time with His creatures is one of the unique aspects of the Christian faith. The gods who have been created by the ingenuity of man's mind have always been gods who are far removed from man's daily life. The mythical gods of the ancient Greek and Roman world had to be placated or feared. The idea of having a close personal relationship with those gods did not exist.

On the other hand, Jesus indicated that the desire of the entire Trinity—God the Father, Son, and Holy Spirit—was to abide or make Their home with the one who responds to God's love.[7] Again, Jesus promised never to leave His followers orphans but told them that He would be with them forever.

In Jesus' prayer to His Father about His own earthly ministry, He said, "Father, I want those you have given me to be with me where I am, and to see my glory, the glory you have given me because you loved me before the creation of the world."[8] Clearly, Jesus desired quality time with all of those who responded to His love.

QUALITY TIME
AS PRACTICED BY JESUS

Jesus illustrated the concept of quality time as an expression of God's love by the design of His own earthly ministry. He preached to the multitudes, but He spent quality time with twelve men. To use the words of The Gospel According to Mark, "He appointed twelve . . . that they might be with him."[9] Later, He appointed them as apostles to carry on His ministry. In order to prepare them for this, Jesus knew that they had to be convinced of God's love for mankind, so He gave them quality time.

Speaking the love language of quality time, Jesus focused attention on these twelve men. Jesus did not attempt to make His ministry as *broad* as possible but rather as *deep* as possible. He wanted these men to experience His love at the deepest possible level.

To use a contemporary expression, Jesus *hung with* the disciples for three and one-half years. They shared meals, travels, experiences, and extended conversations. He taught the multitudes in parables, but it was the Twelve to whom He gave the fuller explanation of the parables in response to their questions. It was clear that Jesus gave quality time to the twelve whom He chose to be apostles.

SPEAKING THE LOVE
LANGUAGE OF QUALITY TIME

Two Sisters

Of course, other individuals also spent quality time with
Jesus. On one occasion, Jesus and His disciples traveled to
the village of Bethany. A woman by the name of Martha invited them into her house, to visit with her and a sister, Mary.

After the formality of greetings, Martha busied herself in
the kitchen preparing a meal for Jesus and His disciples while
Mary sat with the disciples, enthralled with the teaching of
Jesus. Martha became disturbed that her sister was not helping her with preparations for the meal. She became so agi-
tated that she actually entered the room, interrupted Jesus, and
asked Him if He would please encourage her sister to help
her.

Jesus did not condemn Martha for her acts of service,
nor did He condemn Mary for giving Him her undivided
attention. Jesus knew the heart of both sisters. Martha was
concerned about doing the proper thing; but her spirit was
not one of love but rather of agitation. She was, in fact, dis-
tracted from developing a love relationship with Jesus and was
operating from a sense of duty. My guess is that Martha's love
language was acts of service and Mary's was quality time, both
of which can be valid expressions of one's love to God.

On this occasion, however, Martha's attention seems to be
directed to ritual rather than relationship. She put performance above the person of Christ. She was doing what came
natural for her—acts of service—but her heart was not in it.
In much the same way, those whose primary love language
is words of affirmation can often speak empty religious words

with no conscious love toward God. All auth'
God flows from a heart that genuinely see'

George Mueller

Beyond Jesus' day, history is replete with individuals whose primary love language was quality time and who expressed their love to God by spending what to others would have been inordinate amounts of time in prayer, Scripture reading, meditation, and undistracted attention on God. George Mueller was one of those persons. Born in Germany in 1805, Mueller dedicated himself at age twenty entirely to the service of God. He was a theology student at the University at Halle then and would go on to master six languages: Latin, Greek, Hebrew, German, French, and English.

From the beginning of his ministry, Mueller refused any salary for himself and refused to solicit contributions for the ministries which he started. He believed that faith in God and reliance on prayer would provide all his needs. His ministry included free distribution of Bibles and other Christian literature, Christian day schools for the poor, and, most notably, orphanages, which by 1875 lodged, fed, and educated over two thousand English children. His purpose in running orphanages was twofold. In his own words,

> I certainly did from my heart desire to be used by God to
> benefit the bodies of poor children bereaved of both parents,
> and seek in other respects with the help of God to do them
> good for this life. I also particularly longed to be used by
> God in getting the dear orphans trained up in the fear of
> God; but still, the first and primary object of the work was
> and still is that God might be magnified by the fact that the

orphans under my care are provided with all they need, only by prayer and faith without anyone being asked by me or my fellow laborers, whereby it may be seen that God is faithful still, and hears prayer still.[10]

Even before Mueller started orphanages, his lifestyle was characterized by extended periods of quality time with God. The following are excerpts from his diary.

- July 18, 1832: "Today I spent all morning in the vestry, to procure a quiet season. This has been for some time the only way, on account of the multiplicity of engagements, to make sure of time for prayer, reading the word, and meditation."
- July 19, 1832: "I spent from half past nine till one in the vestry. Had real communion with the Lord. The Lord be praised, who has put it into my mind to use the vestry for a place of retirement!"
- June 25, 1834: "These last three days, I have had very little real communion with God, and have therefore been very weak spiritually, and have several times felt irritability of temper."
- June 26, 1834: "I was enabled, by the grace of God, to rise early, and I had nearly two hours in prayer before breakfast. I feel now this morning more comfortable."
- September 29, 1835: "Last evening when I retired from the family, I had a desire to go to rest at once, for I had prayed a short while before; and feeling weak in body, the coldness of the night was a temptation to me to pray no further. However, the Lord did help me to fall upon my knees; and no sooner had I commenced to praying than he shone into my soul, and gave me such a spirit of prayer as I have not

enjoyed in many weeks. He graciously once more revived his work in my heart. I enjoyed that nearness to God and fervency in prayer for more than an hour, for which my soul had been panting for many weeks past. . . . I went to bed especially happy, and awoke this morning in great peace, rose sooner than usual, and had again, for more than an hour, real communion with the Lord before breakfast. May he in mercy continue this state of heart to his most unworthy child."[11]

For George Mueller, quality time with God was the center of his life. It was on these occasions that he sensed deeply the presence and peace of God. Without this quality time, he experienced a sense of distance between God and himself. (He warned fellow believers that "often the work of the Lord itself may be a temptation to keep us from that communion with him which is so essential to the benefit of our own souls.")[12] After being sick for three months and unable to minister, he wrote on January 14, 1838: "I have spent several hours in prayer today, and read on my knees, and prayed for two hours over Psalm 63. God has blessed my soul much today. My soul is now brought into that state that I delight myself in the will of God, as it regards my health."[13] Clearly Mueller's quality times with God were not ritualistic but deep and personal. It affected the whole of his life and was at the center of his love relationship with God.

On May 7, 1841, he wrote: "Now, I saw the most important thing I had to do was to give myself to reading the word of God, and to meditation on it; thus my heart might be comforted, encouraged, warned, reproved, instructed; and that thus, by means of the word of God, whilst meditating on it, my heart might be brought into experimental communion with the Lord."[14] It was this "experimental communion with the Lord" that enabled Mueller to do his ministry.

Looking back on the life of Mueller over a hundred years ago, many are inclined to praise him for his work with orphans and the establishment of schools for the poor of England. Contemporary Christians are enamored that he did this without the solicitation of funds which is so common to philanthropic endeavors in our generation. For Mueller, however, all of this was simply the outgrowth of his quality time with God. Communion with God was far more important in his mind than caring for the poor. "This I most firmly believe," he once wrote, "that no one ought to expect to see much good resulting from his labors in word, and doctrine, if he is not much given to prayer and meditation."[15]

Although his life was characterized by acts of service and words of affirmation for the benefit of others, for Mueller quality time was his primary love language. He spoke it fluently as he developed his love relationship with God.

QUALITY TIME WITH GOD . . .
FOR VISION AND ENERGY

For many individuals, both contemporaries of Mueller and those who have read of his life and ministry in ensuing years, such extended times of communion with God seem incomprehensible. Some say he was a "supersaint," driven to please God. Others have sought to explain Mueller's lifestyle by focusing on the culture in which he lived. One hundred seventy-five years ago life was much simpler. People moved at a slower pace. There was more time for meditation and contemplation.

While this is certainly true, Mueller was one of the busiest men of his generation. Imagine the time involved in administrating numerous orphanages in various locations and numerous schools for the poor children of the cities. Clearly the demands on Mueller's time would have been as great as any modern-day administrator. A better explanation, it seems to me, is that Mueller experienced the love of God most deeply when he spent quality time with God. It is here that Mueller drew not only his vision but his energy. It was in these times of contemplation that he focused on listening to the voice of God through Scripture that Mueller was energized to carry on the ministry to which he was called.

When one's primary love language is quality time, uninterrupted times of communion with God are not difficult but joyous, not burdensome but burden lifting. As Mueller said, "The first great and primary business to which I ought to attend every day is to have my soul happy in the Lord. The first thing to be concerned about is not how much I might serve the Lord, how I might glorify the Lord; but how I might get my soul into a happy state, and how my inner man might be nourished."[16]

SPEAKING THEIR NATIVE TONGUE

For Mueller and thousands like him, quality time is their native tongue. It is their most natural way of experiencing the love of God and reciprocating. Recently, a woman said to me, "I feel closest to God when I have my daily quiet time with Him. It is the most important part of my day. When I miss that time, my whole day seems empty and I don't feel as close to God. It is in those personal times with Him that I feel His love. I know He loves me even when I miss my quiet time, but I don't feel His love." This is not true of everyone, but it is certainly true of those individuals for whom quality time is their primary love language.

Space does not permit the consideration of scores of others whose primary love language was quality time. Four who come to mind are David Brainard, E. M. Bounds, Charles Finney, and Praying Hyde.[17] For them, the words of the following hymn by C. Austin Miles expresses their sentiments:

> I come to the garden alone,
> While the dew is still on the roses;
> And the voice I hear, falling on my ear,
> The Son of God discloses.
> He speaks and the sound of His voice
> Is so sweet the birds hush their singing,
> And the melody that He gave to me
> Within my heart is ringing.
> And He walks with me, and He talks with me,
> And He tells me I am His own;
> And the joy we share as we tarry there
> None other has ever known.[18]

Those who seek quality time with God will learn that He is always ready, waiting to meet with them. Quality time is one of God's great love languages.

4

GOD SPEAKS LOVE LANGUAGE #3: *Gifts*

*Y*EARS AGO, BEFORE THE DAYS of Interstate 20, it was a long trip from North Carolina to Fort Worth, Texas. I had chosen the "southern route" because I wanted to go through Longview, Texas. The previous summer, I had read the autobiography of R. G. LeTourneau, *Mover of Men and Mountains;* now I wanted to meet this engineering genius, manufacturer of earth-moving equipment, who designed his life around a unique partnership with God.

I had driven all night and reached the outskirts of Longview about 9:00 A.M. Stopping to refuel, I asked the attendant, "Can you tell me how to get to the manufacturing plant owned by R. G. LeTourneau?"

"You mean that rich Christian fool?" the attendant asked.

"Why do you say that?" I responded.

"Because he gives away 90 percent of everything he makes. That doesn't make sense to me."

R. G. LeTourneau didn't make sense to a lot of people. In the 1920s, he was more than once the laughingstock of highly trained engineers. He only finished the eighth grade and never had a course in engineering. Yet in the 1960s, he had the distinction of having built the largest earth-moving equipment in the world. His philosophy was, "There are no big jobs; only small machines."[1] During World War II, his earth-moving machines became the "secret weapons" of the war. After the war, he received the tenth annual award of the National Defense Transportation Association as the person whose "achievement contributed most to the effectiveness of the transportation industry in support of national security."[2]

He was a man of dreams with an inventive genius unparalleled by engineers of his day. He once said, "I guess it's good that I never got an education because they might have taught me that my ideas wouldn't work."

THE SECRETS OF HIS SUCCESS

LeTourneau attributed all of his success to two factors. First, God had gifted him with the love of machines. He sometimes feared that his obsession with machines was taking him away from his love of God. But as a young man, he came to understand, "I was just His follower and as long as I ... didn't get to thinking I was operating under my own head of steam, I was on the right track."[3]

Second, he made a conscious decision to make God his partner in business. Having struggled with the idea of being a missionary, he was challenged by his pastor who said, "God needs businessmen as well as preachers and missionaries." So in the middle of the Great Depression and $100,000 in debt, he made God his partner in business. In spite of his huge debt, that year he pledged $5,000 to his church's missionary efforts.

By the mid-1930s, R. G. LeTourneau's small manufacturing operation was beginning to go big time. He had erased his debt, and when he realized that profits would be a half million dollars, he said to his wife, "I think we've got to do more."

"What's on your mind?" his wife, Evelyn, asked. He explained that in the Old Testament, people were required to tithe their income.

"Now, we aren't compelled to give to God," R. G. noted. "It's all voluntary. The only thing is, when you consider what God has done for us, we ought to do better for Him out of gratitude than the doubters had to do by law."[4]

Evelyn and he decided to give half of the stock of the company to a foundation. They further agreed to give half of the company's annual earnings to the foundation and to give half of their own personal income to Christian endeavors around the world. As he put it to his attorney, "I want you to set up a foundation for us. The foundation will sponsor religious, missionary, and educational work for the greater glory of God. I don't know what the laws are, but I want you to fix it so that the funds of the foundation can never be used for company or personal purposes."

His attorney's response? "You're out of your mind, but then you always were."[5] (When the service station attendant said to me, "You mean that rich Christian fool?" I knew it was not an original idea.)

JOY IN GIVING

Later LeTourneau would give 90 percent of the common

stock of his company to the foundation and 90 percent of his personal income to Christian causes around the world. His many donations funded a Christian camp (in Winona Lake, Indiana), two Christian colleges (in Toccoa, Georgia, and Longview, Texas), and two multimillion-dollar mission projects, one in Liberia and the other in Peru. His life was characterized by giving. His greatest joy was in giving back to God. His happiness came from accomplishing things for God by his giving.

In 1942, when the company's net earnings topped the two-million-dollar mark for the first time, he reflected on the early beginnings when he had made his $5,000 pledge to the missions fund while in debt $100,000. When he was asked, "Are you happier now than you were then?" his response was, "More grateful, perhaps, because God has let us help Him do some of the things we wanted to do then. But happier? We had been in the service of the Lord then, and we are in the service of the Lord now, and there is nothing in that kind of happiness that two million net earnings can add to, or buy."[6]

LeTourneau's obsession with giving seemed strange to many of his contemporaries, and perhaps to some who read this account. But it is not strange to those whose primary love language is gifts. For LeTourneau, it was the most logical thing in the world. He viewed all of life as a gift from God. This is clearly seen as one reads his biography. He saw his fascination with machines as a gift from God. When he would go back to the drawing board to design some new earth-moving monster after dinner at night, he never thought of it as working but rather as a chance to "play with my big toys." Time was viewed as a gift from God to be treated respectfully and gratefully. He once said, "If you waste dollars for me—it is not too serious. I can make that up. But don't waste my time—it can't be recalled."[7]

As a young man, LeTourneau was very reticent to speak publicly, but in his later years he spoke to hundreds of thousands. His speech always began with the same introduction: "I'm just a mechanic that God has blessed, and He has blessed me—a sinner saved by grace." The word *grace* is a Greek word which literally means "unmerited favor." LeTourneau saw himself as a recipient of God's unmerited favor. He saw himself "saved" from a life of meaningless activity to a life of fruitfulness in cooperating with God as his partner.

The "inner peace" that came to him at the age of sixteen was the result of God's grace. Here is his description of what happened that night. "No bolts of lightning hit me. No great flash of awareness. I just prayed to the Lord to save me, and then I was aware of another presence. No words were spoken. I received no messages. It was just that all of my bitterness was drained away, and I was filled with such a vast relief that I could not contain it all. I ran to my mother. 'I'm saved,' I cried."[8]

Because LeTourneau saw his relationship with God as a gift bestowed upon him, he also viewed his money as a gift from God. He had a deep concern for the people of the whole world. When confronted with other cultures, his questions were always the same. "How much have they got to eat? How comfortably are they housed? What assurance have they got of a life eternal?" He noted in his autobiography, "I know that in the jungles of Africa and South America, the advancements of science make fine reading, but good food, shelter, and the immediate presence of Christ give life its full richness, now and hereafter. I think that is true everywhere."[9] It is clear that LeTourneau's missionary efforts were expressions of his love for people because of his own experience of the love of God.

LeTourneau's life could be characterized as a love relationship with God. Here is his way of expressing it.

I have learned that God is love, and love wants to be loved. That is why He made us with His attributes, and so gave us the power to love and to hate, the power to choose between good and evil and say "I will" or "I will not." God loves the sinner, but He hates sin. He made the universe, and all living things in it, and pronounced it good. But He wasn't satisfied yet. He said, "Let us make man in Our own image and in Our own likeness." So He breathed into man the breath of life, and man became a living soul. I believe . . . that God wanted a creature so like Himself that He could always be in fellowship with him.

That privilege of fellowship with Him is a reward beyond comprehension, but He does not stop there. When you come to love Him and serve Him, then all else is yours, now and forevermore. I believe that when I have done what I can for Him down here, He will change this body of mine "that it may be fashioned like unto His glorious body" (Philippians 3:21). Not because I was so good, but because the Lord Jesus Christ was good enough to die for me, and I accepted His offer of salvation and have been born again into the family of God (John 3:16). That same offer is open to all. No greater can ever be made.[10]

When one understands that R.G. LeTourneau viewed all of life as an expression of God's love for him, then one begins to understand why LeTourneau often said, "The question is not how much of my money I give to God, but rather how much of God's money I keep for myself."[11]

GOD, THE GREAT GIFT-GIVER

LeTourneau's perception of God as the great gift-giver

is indeed the God we discover in the Hebrew Old Testament and the Greek New Testament. The opening chapter of the Hebrew Scriptures reads:

> *So God created man in his own image, in the image of God he created him; male and female he created them. . . . Then God said, "I give you every seed-bearing plant on the face of the whole earth and every tree that has fruit with seed in it. They will be yours for food. And to all the beasts of the earth and all the birds of the air and all the creatures that move on the ground—everything that has the breath of life in it—I give every green plant for food." And it was so.*
>
> *God saw all that he had made, and it was very good.*[12]

Compare this picture of God as the "gift-giver" at the dawn of creation with the following words from the last chapter in the Bible, describing the second coming of Jesus Christ and the beginning of a new age:

> *"Behold I am coming soon! My reward is with me . . . I am the Alpha and the Omega, the First and the Last, the Beginning and the End. Blessed are those who wash their robes, that they may have the right to the tree of life and may go through the gates into the city. . . .*
>
> *"I am the Root and the Offspring of David, and the bright Morning Star."*
>
> *The Spirit and the bride say, "Come!" And let him who hears say, "Come!" Whoever is thirsty, let him come; and whoever wishes, let him take the free gift of the water of life.*[13]

Throughout the Scriptures, God reveals Himself as the gift-giver. Moses, whom God used to deliver Israel from the bondage of Egyptian slavery, said of God: "He will love you and bless you and increase your numbers. He will bless the fruit of your womb, the crops of your land—your grain, new wine and oil—the calves of your herds and the lambs of your flocks in the land that he swore to your forefathers to give you."[14]

Clearly God had established a love relationship with ancient Israel. He provided them with the guidelines to a meaningful and fruitful life. In following these guidelines, they were expressing their trust and love in Jehovah. He, in turn, would shower them with gifts of love. Their reciprocal covenant relationship with God is depicted in the following words spoken by Moses: "So if you faithfully obey the commands I am giving you today—to love the LORD your God and to serve him with all your heart and with all your soul—then I will send rain on your land in its season, both autumn and spring rains, so that you may gather in your grain, new wine and oil. I will provide grass in the fields for your cattle, and you will eat and be satisfied."[15]

A RECIPROCAL, PERSONAL LOVE

This reciprocal love relationship, expressed in giving gifts, is also seen on the personal level. God expressed His love to Solomon, the young king of Israel, by asking, "What shall I give you?" Hebrew history records that God gave much more than Solomon requested:

"Now, O LORD my God, you have made your servant king in place of my father David. But I am only a little child and do not know how to carry out my duties.... So give your servant a discerning heart to govern your people and to distinguish between right and wrong. For who is able to govern this great people of yours?"

God, the great giver of gifts, responded. "Since you have asked for this and not for long life or wealth for yourself, nor have asked for the death of your enemies but for discernment in administrating justice, I will do what you have asked. I will give you a wise and discerning heart, so that there will never have been anyone like you, nor will there ever be. Moreover, I will give you what you have not asked for—both riches and honor—so that in your lifetime you will have no equal among kings."[16]

Many of the Hebrew songs captured this picture of God as the great gift-giver; for example, Psalm 5:12: "For surely, O LORD, you bless the righteous; you surround them with your favor as with a shield."

GIFTS TO THOSE WHO LOVE HIM

The New Testament continues painting the portrait of the God of love who freely gives gifts to those who love Him. Many agree that the message of the Bible can be summarized in one verse, namely, John 3:16: "For God so loved the world that he gave his one and only Son, that whoever believes in him shall not perish but have eternal life."

What many have not understood is that these words were spoken by Jesus. He was identifying Himself as God's one and only Son and proclaiming His mission on earth. Jesus continued, "For God did not send his Son into the world to condemn the world, but to save the world through him. . . . The Father loves the Son and has placed everything in his hands. Whoever believes in the Son has eternal life, but whoever rejects the Son will not see life, for God's wrath remains on him."[17]

Gifts Promised by Jesus

The teachings of Jesus were permeated with the concept that God wants to give good gifts to those who love Him. Before Jesus was ever arrested in Jerusalem, He said to His followers, "In a little while you will see me no more, and then after a little while you will see me . . . because I am going to the Father. . . . I tell you the truth, you will weep and mourn while the world rejoices. You will grieve, but your grief will turn to joy."[18]

The message was clear. Jesus was going to die, and after His resurrection He would return to His Father where He was before His birth as a babe in Bethlehem. But He wanted His followers to know that God would continue to give good gifts to them. He said, "In that day, you will no longer ask me anything. I tell you the truth, my Father will give you whatever you ask in my name. . . . Ask and you will receive, and your joy will be complete."[19]

Gifts Declared by the Apostles

Much of the New Testament was written by Saul of Tarsus, a well-educated Jewish zealot who, in his earlier years, tried to stamp out those who were followers of Christ. He sincerely endeavored to eradicate what he considered to be a violation of the Jewish faith. But after his conversion to Christ, he became an ardent apostle—first to the Jews and then to the Gentiles—proclaiming that Jesus was indeed the Messiah prophesied by Israel's prophets, and in Him was the gift of eternal life.

Paul's message reflected the covenant love relationship between God and His creatures. Paul once said, "Be imitators of God, therefore, as dearly loved children and live a life of love, just as Christ loved us and gave himself up for us as a fragrant offering and sacrifice."[20]

Two other apostles saw God as the great gift-giver. "Every good and perfect gift is from above, coming down from the Father of the heavenly lights, who does not change like shifting shadows," wrote the apostle James; and John noted, "How great is the love the Father has lavished on us, that we should be called the children of God!" Perhaps God's greatest gift is our being remade in Christ upon His return. "Dear friends, now we are children of God, and what we will be has not yet been made known. But we know that when he appears, we shall be like him."[21]

Throughout human history, God has revealed Himself as one who loves those who will acknowledge Him. He, in turn, expresses His love by giving gifts. Often those gifts are material things that can be touched and tasted, such things as food, clothing, and shelter. On other occasions, His gifts are in the realm of the spiritual—the gift of eternal life, forgiveness of sins, peace of mind, and purpose of life.

Among those spiritual gifts are those given to the first-century church, especially the early gifts of leadership—"some to be apostles . . . prophets . . . evangelists, and . . . pastors and teachers." These gifts to the church were to prepare God's people, so that the work of Christ on earth could continue.[22]

Since those early days of the Christian faith, every believer in Christ has been given distinct "spiritual gifts," abilities to perform certain tasks in the body of Christ. These gifts include such things as wisdom, knowledge, faith, gifts of healing, prophecy, distinguishing between spirits, and leadership skills. These gifts are given by God "for the common good."[23]

These various gifts have allowed the followers of Christ to carry on the work of Christ for two thousand years.

THOSE WHOSE PRIMARY
LOVE LANGUAGE IS GIFTS

The theme of God as the giver of gifts runs deeply through the channels of Hebrew and Christian history. To those individuals for whom gift-giving is the primary love language, this aspect of God's nature has been extremely compelling. When they think of God, they think of Him as the one who gives good gifts.

Meet Monica

Monica was twenty-six when I met her. She attended one of my seminars and on Saturday morning brought me a gift: a loaf of freshly baked wheat bread. In the course of our conversation, she said, "Three years ago I was not a Christian. My parents sent me to church when I was a child, but my father was an alcoholic and my mother was very demanding. At sixteen I ran away from home and never returned. I lived my life doing what I wanted to do. Because my parents said they were Christians, I knew that I wanted nothing to do with the church or God."

For seven years she devoted her life to seeking pleasure, through sex, alcohol, and eventually hard drugs. There was no happiness in this, she said, and eventually she found herself in a drug treatment center operated by Teen Challenge Ministries.

"It was there that I heard for the first time that God loved me," Monica told me. "I learned that because Jesus had paid the penalty for my sins by dying on the cross, God would forgive me and give me the gift of eternal life. At first I could not believe what I was hearing. I thought of God as the judge who demanded perfection and who cursed those who did not obey His laws. I never pictured Him as a God who loved me and wanted to give me anything. I could not imagine that He could forgive me for all the things I had done, accept me into His family, and let me live forever with Him in heaven.

"It was too good to be true. I resisted the idea for several weeks.

"As I read the Scriptures for myself, one night I cried out to God and said, 'If it is true, if You really love me, then I'm asking You to forgive me and I'm inviting You into my life. If You can clean up my life and deliver me from drug addiction and give me the gift of eternal life, I am willing to accept Your love.' My life changed that night, and I know I will never be the same again."

Monica completed the program, and Teen Challenge referred her to a group of Christians, who, in turn, invited her to live with them. She found they genuinely cared for each other. Two weeks later, "they gave me the first birthday cake I had had since I was twelve," she said. "Here were people, themselves former addicts, who had accepted God's love and were now giving His love to others."

She met Bill there; they fell in love and were married a year before the seminar. As she explained it, "Because God has given so much to me, my ministry is baking bread and giving it to others. Every week I bake twenty loaves of bread and distribute them to people whom God brings into my life."

I embraced Monica and Bill, thanked God for His gifts to them, and then prayed His blessing upon their marriage.

Monica is a living example that God speaks the love language of gifts.

Throughout history, thousands of individuals whose primary love language is gifts have been drawn to Him because He stands not as a judge to condemn but as a Father who wants to give forgiveness and eternal life to those who will receive His love.

Maria's Pastor

When an individual's primary love language is gifts, he or she will tend to express love to God by giving gifts. I remember Maria, a young wife in California, who said to me, "When I read your book *The Five Love Languages,* I was especially attracted to the chapter on gifts because that is my primary love language. I started thinking about other people whose love language might be gifts.

"It was interesting the names that came to my mind. I remember the pastor of our first church when we moved to California. His language was definitely gifts. He gave us a piano the first month we arrived at the church. He was always bringing vegetables to our house, sometimes vegetables which other people had given to him. He was always asking, 'What do you need?' It seemed he couldn't give us enough.

"I knew his love language was gifts, and we were the recipients of his love. When we would say 'Thank you,' he would say, 'Don't thank me; thank God. All good gifts come from Him.'"

It was clear to me that Maria's pastor was expressing his love to God when he gave gifts to people in his congregation. I was sure that if I could have talked with him, he would probably have quoted to me the words of Jesus when He described the final judgment.

>—<

"Then the King will say to those on his right, 'Come, you who are blessed by my Father; take your inheritance, the kingdom prepared for you since the creation of the world. For I was hungry and you gave me something to eat, I was thirsty and you gave me something to drink, I was a stranger and you invited me in, I needed clothes and you clothed me, I was sick and you looked after me, I was in prison and you came to visit me.'

"Then the righteous will answer him, 'Lord, when did we see you hungry and feed you, or thirsty and give you something to drink? When did we see you a stranger and invited you in, or needing clothes and clothe you? When did we see you sick or in prison and go to visit you?'

"The King will reply, 'I tell you the truth, whatever you did for one of the least of these brothers of mine, you did for me.'"[24]

The message of Jesus was clear. One of the ways of expressing our love to God is by giving gifts to those who need them.

It is this truth that deeply motivates followers of Jesus. As one man said to me, "I never feel more joy than when I am giving to others. I feel like this is why God has given to me, and it is the way I can express my love to Him." Another man said, "I feel closest to God when I am taking care of His creatures by giving them what they cannot provide for themselves." For these people, giving is a way of life.

Anne's Gifts

When I think of giving gifts as an expression of one's love for God, the first person who comes to my mind is Anne Wenger. I knew her for over twenty-five years. She was a speech pathologist but had herself suffered from polio and walked haltingly. When she stopped working publicly, people would bring children to her house for speech therapy. She gave freely of her time and expertise, but no child ever left her house without a gift. It may have been as simple as a piece of literature she thought would be helpful to them or an apple from the fruit basket in the kitchen near her chair. Her door was never locked; people came and went from her house regularly.

A young college student who lived in the basement apartment mowed Anne's grass. Others from the church volunteered to vacuum her floors and mop the kitchen. The youth group kept her leaves raked each fall. Everyone was happy to do something for Anne Wenger, perhaps because they had all been the recipients of her gifts.

In my own personal experience, I never left Anne's presence without something in my hand, usually a book or booklet that she thought would help me in my own ministry to others. I remember one of the last times I visited in her home, a few weeks before she went to live in the nursing facility. She said, "I'm giving away my possessions while I'm still alive because I want them to go to people whom I think will use them. I want your son Derek to have this set of books." She pointed to a thirty-five-volume set, the Library of the World's Best Literature.

I said to her, "Anne, I know he would be happy to receive them, but I want you to check with your daughter first and make sure that she doesn't want them. I wouldn't want Derek to have them if Elizabeth wanted them."

Anne nodded her head and said, "You're right. That's a good idea. Let me ask Elizabeth."

Two weeks later I got a call from Anne. "You can come and pick up the books," she said. "I talked with Elizabeth and she wants Derek to have them." And so I did.

Over the next several months, as I visited Anne in the nursing home, her pattern of giving did not waver. She had almost no material possessions at this point, but as I got ready to leave her room, she would say, "Here, take this lotion home to Karolyn. I know she can use it." And she would give me a small container of lotion, probably one that had been given to her by someone else.

Anne Wenger was a giver who is remembered by hundreds of individuals who received tokens of her love through the years.

In my conversations with Anne over twenty-five years, she spoke deeply of the love of God which she experienced in her own life. She saw God as the great gift-giver and her gifts to others as the reflection of His love through her.

HOW WE RECEIVE GIFTS FROM GOD

How does one receive God's gift of love? Some gifts are given indiscriminately by God to everyone. The rising and setting of the sun, the gentle rain, spring flowers, the birds, and the seasons are all God's gifts dispensed to mankind. The psalmist wrote, "The heavens declare the glory of God; the skies proclaim the work of his hands. Day after day they pour forth speech; night after night they display knowledge. There is no speech or language where their voice is not heard."[25] As parents provide for the basic needs of their children—food, clothing, and shelter—so God provides for His creatures day after day.

ASKING AND RECEIVING

However, others of God's gifts are reserved for those who ask. Jesus once said, "Ask and it will be given to you; seek and you will find; knock and the door will be opened to you. For everyone who asks receives; he who seeks finds; and to him who knocks, the door will be opened." Then Jesus explained why we could count on God to give us good gifts. "Which of you, if his son asks for bread, will give him a stone? Or if he asks for a fish, will give him a snake? If you, then, though you are evil, know how to give good gifts to your children, how much more will your Father in heaven give good gifts to those who ask him!"[26]

I have always found it astounding that the eternal God would invite us to ask Him for gifts, but that is precisely what Jesus taught. This does not mean that God will give us exactly what we ask for, every time we ask. A wise parent will not give a child three candy bars even though the child may ask. The promise is that God will give us "good gifts" when we ask. Parents would not give a child something they knew to be destructive even though the child asked intently, nor would God. He loves us too much for that.

The apostle James also indicated another reason God does not always give us exactly what we ask. "When you ask, you do not receive, because you ask with wrong motives, that you may spend what you get on your pleasures."[27] Hedonistic requests that focus on selfish pleasure as the chief good in life will obviously not be answered by God. He loves us too much to enable us to build our lives on a false premise.

Receiving and Giving

When we are rightly related to God, our desire is to receive from Him His gifts in order that we may give to others. Thus a pastor prays for wisdom in shepherding his flock; a parent prays for emotional and physical strength to perform parenting responsibilities. If we ask for material possessions, which is not discouraged in the Scriptures, it is for the purpose of using these to enhance our ministry to others. Possessing material things simply for the sake of possessing is foreign to the biblical concept of love. "How may I use what God gives me to minister to others?" is the question asked by the sincere follower of Jesus.

As God gives to us, we become channels of His love to others. The parent may pray for tuition money to send a daughter to college. When it comes, the money is invested in enriching the child's life. If God gives more than is needed, we can use it to enrich the life of someone else's child. Monies not needed to meet the needs of our family can be given to support the work of missionaries and pastors around the world. We express our love to God by loving others. We receive the gifts of wisdom, insight, experience, expertise, and material possessions to enrich the lives of other people.

The word *gift* comes from the Greek word *charis,* which means "unmerited favor." God's gifts are never given because we deserve them; they are given as expressions of His love for us. Thus, our gifts to others are not based upon the person's performance or what the individual has done for us, but rather flow from our love for the person.

God speaks the love language of gift-giving fluently. When we give to others, we reflect His love.

5

GOD SPEAKS LOVE LANGUAGE #4:
Acts of Service

*J*T WAS THE WEEK BETWEEN Christmas and New Year's Day, and Paul Brown (not his real name) was in my office for his annual "checkup." For over fifteen years, I've known that the week after Christmas Paul would call my secretary and ask for an appointment. A high school math teacher in another city, Paul spends part of his week of freedom with me.

As he sat down, he looked the same as last year. Perhaps his beard was a little bushier, his hair a little longer, his stomach a little bigger, and his clothes draped a little more loosely on his body. He began as he always begins. With my answers interlaced, he asked, "How's your son? . . . How's your daughter? . . . How's your wife?" His mode was sincere and he listened as I gave my report.

Then he said what he always says—"Well, let's cut to the

chase"—and, pulling a piece of crumpled paper from one pocket and a pen from the other, he asked me the same question he always asks: "How do you know when it's God's will for you to get married?"

Paul is forty-two and has never been married, though he's been dating Becky for twelve years, and they were friends seven years before they started dating. "Why do you ask that question?" I inquired, with a clinical look on my face.

"Well, Becky has said, 'Don't bother to come around anymore if you are not willing to talk marriage.' I don't know if I'm ready for that. My lifestyle doesn't lend itself to marriage. I work seventy-five hours a week, and I don't think most wives would put up with that."

I nodded and asked, "Tell me your daily schedule."

"Well, officially my day starts at 8:30 A.M., but I usually get there an hour earlier. I teach from 8:30 till 3:30, and then I tutor individual students from 3:30 till 10:30 at night and sometimes later. You know they give me the worst kids in the school. Some of them can't do basic math. They are the kind of kids that aren't going to get it in the classroom; but when I get them one-on-one, there's no faking it, and they learn. You know, it's not cool to ask questions in class. They act like they understand when I know they don't. They can't graduate from high school without passing the algebra exam, and they are never going to do that without individual help.

"I don't mind putting in the time. Of course, I don't get paid for it, but I don't think a wife would understand."

PLACING THE DECIMAL

I found out Paul had been keeping this schedule for seven years. None of the other math teachers did, of course. But as he explained, "They have the cream of the crop. They can explain it in class, and their students get it, but my students simply can't 'get it' in class. You have to understand. I'm dealing with kids who don't understand the basics. They're still trying to figure out which way to move the decimal if you want to go to a percentage. Is it left or right?

"Let me tell you something God gave me," Paul continued. "I'm not bragging; it just came to me one day. I prayed, 'Lord, how can I help these students understand and remember which way to move the decimal?' So I wrote the alphabet on the board—A, B, C, D . . . right on down through P. I underlined D and P. I pointed to the D and I said, 'Now, if you've got a decimal and you want to make it a percentage (I pointed to the P), which way do you move the decimal?'

"They said, 'To the right.' Then I went to the P and said, 'Now if you've got a percentage and you want to translate it to a decimal, which way do you move the decimal?' I pointed to the D.

"'To the left,' they shouted. I knew they had it. So when I get their exams three weeks later, they actually had the alphabet written across the top of the exam paper with the D and the P underlined."

We both laughed; then Paul said, "It's a challenge, but I know I'm making a difference in their lives. They will graduate from high school because I took the time to help them. You see, I don't have any discipline problems in my classroom. The students know that I am on their side. They say to each other, 'Don't bother Mr. B; he's one of us.'"

CUTTING BACK THE HOURS

I leaned back in my chair and said, "Paul, I think you're

right. I don't think any wife would be happy with her husband working seventy-five hours a week. So let's imagine that you are married and you had to cut back the hours. What would be the possibilities?"

"Well, I'd need a full-time assistant who could tutor the students after class. In fact, I told the principal one day, 'You need to hire me as a full-time tutor. Let somebody else teach the classes, and I'll work from 3:30 until 11:30 P.M. every day, tutoring the students who can't get it in class.' Of course, I know that's not going to happen, but that would be ideal.

"The other thing I've thought about is I could teach math in a college prep school or on the college level. I know they're not going to move me as long as I stay at my present school because the principal is happy with the test scores and so are the parents. So, why would they move me? They know that no one else is going to invest the time I invest with the students. But on the other hand, I'm not sure I want to be transferred. After all, this is what motivated me to go back to the university and get my master's degree. You remember?" He looked at me and I nodded.

I remembered. In fact, I remembered a lot about Paul. I remembered when his mother died with cancer while Paul was still in high school. His mother, a devout Catholic, prayed that God would take care of her seven children. I remembered when Paul went off to college to pursue his vision of becoming a math teacher. In college, Paul became a devout follower of Jesus Christ. He was not concerned about being Catholic or Protestant but about learning and following the teachings of Jesus. I remembered when Paul changed his major from math to communications, a decision made out of a sincere desire to learn how to communicate the teachings of Christ to others.

I remembered the struggles Paul went through for several years after college, working for a communications company but always wondering if this was really what he should be doing with his life. And I remembered distinctly the choice to go back to the university to finish his undergraduate major in math and then to pursue his master's degree so he could teach, which was his original vision and passion.

So I said to Paul, "Do you understand what is going on here? You're living the lifestyle of a monk, devoting your life to teaching math and helping students graduate from high school who otherwise would not make it. Thus, you are making a difference in their lives forever. On the other hand, you have a desire for marriage, but you don't see the two as compatible. It is the choice that thousands of priests and nuns have made through the years. Most of them made the decision much earlier in life, but the decision is the same."

THE POSSIBILITY OF MARRIAGE . . .

I paused and continued, "Maybe it's time for you to realistically explore the possibility of marriage. This might include saying to Becky, 'I'm willing to think about marriage if both of us can realize that the process may not lead to marriage,'" I continued. "This might involve attending some marriage preparation classes. It might involve taking a psychological test which would indicate the level of compatibility between the two of you. It would certainly involve looking at your lifestyles and asking, 'What would things be like if we were married?' It might involve the possibility of exploring change in vocational settings, but at least, at the end of the process, you could make an intelligent decision about marriage."

The room fell silent. I could tell that Paul was contemplating what I had just said. "I'm not sure I'm willing to take those steps," he said. "At least, not at this time." We talked about several other matters of lesser importance. As usual, Paul thanked me for my time and told me how much he appreciated my being a sounding board. As he walked out, I knew I would see him again next Christmas. And, again, we'd talk about "how to know the will of God about marriage."

EXPRESSING LOVE TO GOD
THROUGH ACTS OF SERVICE

Paul's primary love language is acts of service. Tutoring those underachieving math students was his way of expressing his love to God. That's why the thought of walking away from those students, even for the prospects of a marriage relationship, was so difficult for Paul to imagine. However, this was not the first time I had observed Paul's love language. While he was working for the communications company, he volunteered to run the sound system for his local church and to edit the pastor's sermons for local radio. During those years, he consistently spent twenty hours a week in this volunteer service. It was his way of expressing his love to God.

I cannot predict whether Paul will ever get married, but I can predict that if he does he will find a way to serve others, because acts of service is his primary love language.

THE PROPHETESS OF LOVE

Not many of my readers will know Paul Brown, but most of my readers will know Mother Teresa. She is the twentieth century's prophetess of love, and there can be no question that her primary love language was acts of service.

As a teenager, Agnes Bojaxhiu (Mother Teresa's birth name)

joined a Catholic youth group in the Jesuit parish of the Sacred Heart in her home town of Skoplje, Albania. At the age of eighteen, she moved to Ireland to join the Sisters of Our Lady of Loreto. Three months later, she was sent to Calcutta, India, and later to Darjeeling, near the Himalayas, where in 1937 she made permanent vows and took the name "Teresa." After nine years of teaching at the only Catholic school for girls in Calcutta, most of whom were from well-to-do families, Sister Teresa became "aware of a calling in the midst of my vocation: I had to leave the convent (Loreto) and consecrate myself to help the poor, living among them. Abandoning Loreto was an even harder sacrifice than leaving my family that first time in order to follow my vocation. But I had to do it. It was a calling. I knew I had to go; I did not know how to get there."[1]

Some of Mother Teresa's former students followed her, and they formed the nucleus of what became "Missionaries of Charity." Mother Teresa started working with those she found first: abandoned children living in the city parks. She began by teaching them basic habits of good hygiene. She helped them learn the alphabet. She had no master blueprint for her work, but her goal was clear: to love and serve the poor, seeing Jesus in them. She said, "In determining which work would be done, there was no planning at all. I headed the work in accordance with how I felt called by the people's sufferings. God made me see what He wanted me to do."[2]

When she found a woman dying on a sidewalk, she took the woman home with her and shortly thereafter opened the Home for the Dying in order to provide a peaceful and dignified place for people to die. Later, when she found abandoned children, sometimes the sons and daughters of those staying at the Home for the Dying, she opened Shishu Bhaban, the first of a series of children's homes. In similar manner, she started homes for lepers, people with AIDS, and unwed mothers. Awarded the Nobel Peace Prize in 1979, she did not consider the cash award as personal property but accepted it in the name of the poor and spent it all on them.

To view Mother Teresa as simply an unusually altruistic person is to miss the central message of her life: "Whoever the poorest of the poor are, they are Christ for us—Christ under the guise of human suffering. The Missionaries of Charity are firmly convinced that each time we offer help to the poor, we really offer help to Christ." On another occasion, she said, "When we touch the sick and needy, we touch the suffering body of Christ." And again, "Jesus is the one we take care of, visit, clothe, feed, and comfort. Every time we do this for the poorest of the poor, to the sick, to the dying, to the lepers, and to the ones who suffer from AIDS, we should not serve the poor like they *were* Jesus; we should serve the poor because they are Jesus."[3]

SERVING PEOPLE EQUALS LOVING GOD

The central dimension of Mother Teresa's acts of service was spiritual in nature. "To me, Jesus is the Life I want to live, the Light I want to reflect, the Way to the Father, the Love I want to express, the Joy I want to share, the Peace I want to sow around me."[4] For her, serving people was loving God.

Love always involved service and sacrifice for Mother Teresa. After all, she reasoned, this is how God expressed His love to us. "True love causes pain. Jesus, in order to give us the proof of His love, died on the cross. A mother, in order to give birth to her baby, has to suffer. If you really love one another, you will not be able to avoid making sacrifices."[5]

When Mother Teresa challenged others to join her in loving God, it was most often expressed in terms of acts of service. "I invite all those who appreciate our work to look around them and be willing to love those who have no love and to offer them their services. Are we not, by definition, messengers of love?" Later she said, "Let us not be satisfied just by giving money. Money is not everything. The poor need the work of our hands, the love of our hearts. Love, an abundant love, is the expression of our Christian religion."[6]

To those who sought to follow her example, Mother Teresa emphasized the connection between loving people and loving God.

> It happened once, when the Congregation of the Missionary Brothers of Charity was first established, that a young Brother came to me and said, "Mother, I have a special call to work with the lepers. I want to give my life to them, my whole being. Nothing attracts me more than that." I know for a fact that he truly loved those afflicted with leprosy. I, in turn, answered him, "I think that you are somewhat wrong, Brother. Our vocation consists in belonging to Jesus. The work is nothing but a means to express our love for him. The work in itself is not important. What is important is for you to belong to Jesus and he is the one who offers you the means to express that belonging."[7]

For her, caring for spiritual needs was even more important than caring for material needs. "We have the specific task of giving material and spiritual help to the poorest of the poor, not only the ones in the slums but those who live in any corner of the world as well. . . . If our work were just to wash and feed and give medicines to the sick, the center would have closed a long time ago. The most important thing in our centers is the opportunity we are offered to reach the souls."[8]

THE SUPREME ACT OF SERVICE:
A LIFE SACRIFICED

For Mother Teresa, God expressed His love for us by sending His uniquely begotten Son, Jesus, who in turn expressed His love by the supreme act of service: giving His life for our sins. When as a young teenage girl Agnes Bojaxhiu responded to that love, her life course was set. Hers would be a life characterized by compassion, generosity, and selflessness through acts of service to the poor. Her life captured the attention of the world but was intensely personally motivated by her love for Jesus. To thousands of followers of Christ whose primary love language, like hers, is acts of service, she became a model.

GOD'S ACTS OF SERVICE
THROUGH THE YEARS

Who is this God who captured the heart of Agnes Bojaxhiu and turned her into Mother Teresa? The answer is not elusive. He is the God of Abraham, Isaac, Jacob, and Joseph; and the One declared in the Bible as "the God and Father of our Lord Jesus Christ."[9] He is the God who speaks fluently the love language acts of service.

What Jewish child does not know the story of God's act of love in delivering Israel from Egyptian bondage? So important is this act of love that it has been celebrated by the Jewish community for over 3,500 years as Passover.

During their forty-year journey from Egypt to Canaan,

the people of Israel watched God express His love by acts of service on numerous occasions. There was the parting of the Red Sea, made vivid to modern audiences by Cecil B. DeMille's movie *The Ten Commandments.* In the midst of the desert, God provided water to drink and quail and manna to eat. The Jewish nation was so profoundly affected by God's love through acts of service that they often described their history by reciting the mighty acts of God on behalf of Israel.

Unlike Baal and the pagan gods of their neighbors, who never responded to the prayers and sacrifices of those who called on them, Israel's God revealed His love by acts of service in response to the prayers of His people. Enemies were routed, plagues were averted, droughts were ended, and diseases healed when Israel called on God.

The perception of God as the one who acts was so central to Jewish thought that one of the names they attributed to God was *Elohim,* the All Powerful One.

The writer of the Psalms contrasted the God of Israel with pagan gods by emphasizing God's mighty acts of service on behalf of Israel. Speaking of pagan gods, the psalmist wrote, "Their idols are silver and gold, made by the hands of men. They have mouths, but cannot speak, eyes, but they cannot see; they have ears, but cannot hear, noses, but they cannot smell; they have hands, but cannot feel, feet, but they cannot walk; nor can they utter a sound with their throats." In contrast, speaking of the God of Israel, the psalmist says, "O house of Israel, trust in the LORD—he is [our] help and shield. . . . The LORD remembers us and will bless us: he will bless the house of Israel, he will bless the house of Aaron, he will bless those who fear the LORD—small and great alike."[10] Clearly, the God of Israel is the God who expressed His love by acts of service to those who called upon Him.

ACTS OF SERVICE
AND THE WORDS OF JESUS

Yet notice that the focus of Mother Teresa's acts of service was Jesus, not the God Elohim. Why? When we examine the life of Jesus of Nazareth, we find Him identifying Himself with the God of Israel. These claims are so clear and so woven into Jesus' concept of Himself that many have found them incredible and have concluded that Jesus was a man with delusions of grandeur, one not to be seriously considered as a creditable religious leader.

What are these statements of Jesus that have been considered incredible (but that Mother Teresa and countless others have accepted as true)? Early in His adult life, Jesus returned to the village of Nazareth, where He had grown up, and went to the synagogue on the Sabbath. When asked to read the Scriptures, He opened the scroll to Isaiah chapter 61 and read the following: "The Spirit of the Lord is on me, because he has anointed me to preach good news to the poor. He has sent me to proclaim freedom for the prisoners and recovery of sight for the blind, to release the oppressed, to proclaim the year of the Lord's favor."[11]

This passage was commonly understood to be a prophecy of the Messiah who would someday come to Israel. When Jesus completed the reading He said: "Today this scripture is fulfilled in your hearing." Thus, He claimed to be the long-awaited Messiah. So furious were the leaders of the synagogue that they literally forced Jesus out of town. That led Jesus to say, "No prophet is accepted in his hometown."[12] And then Jesus began a three-year ministry filled with acts of service.

On another occasion, Jesus looked toward heaven and prayed. "Father, the time has come. Glorify your Son, that your

Son may glorify you. For you granted him authority over all people that he might give eternal life to all those you have given him." Then He added these words to His sincere prayer: "Now this is eternal life: that they may know you, the only true God, and Jesus Christ, whom you have sent. I have brought you glory on earth by completing the work you gave me to do. And now, Father, glorify me in your presence with the glory I had with you before the world began."[13]

Clearly, Jesus had declared Himself God's unique Son, given great glory in heaven. Now, seeking to prepare His followers for His God-ordained death, Jesus said,

> *"Do not let your hearts be troubled. Trust in God; trust also in me. In my Father's house are many rooms; if it were not so, I would have told you. I am going there to prepare a place for you. And if I go and prepare a place for you, I will come back and take you to be with me that you also may be where I am. You know the way to the place where I am going."*
>
> *Thomas said to him, "Lord, we don't know where you are going, so how can we know the way?"*
>
> *Jesus answered, "I am the way and the truth and the life. No one comes to the Father except through me. If you really knew me, you would know my Father as well."*[14]

Jesus claimed His "acts of service," including preparing "a place" for His followers, were like the loving acts of service by His Father. But His words "If you really knew me, you would know my Father as well" puzzled one of his disciples.

> *Philip said, "Lord, show us the Father and that will be enough for us."*

Jesus answered: "Don't you know me, Philip, even after I have been among you such a long time? Anyone who has seen me has seen the Father. How can you say, 'Show us the Father'? Don't you believe that I am in the Father, and that the Father is in me? The words I say to you are not just my own. Rather, it is the Father living in me who is doing his work. Believe me when I say that I am in the Father and the Father is in me; or at least believe on the evidence of the miracles themselves."[15]

If one begins with the assumption that the Incarnation—God becoming man—is impossible, then it is easy to see why one would find Jesus' teachings to be incredible. However, what is interesting is that Jesus used His acts of service as evidence of the truthfulness of His claims. As He told His disciples, "If I had not done among them what no one else did, they would not be guilty of sin. But now they have seen these miracles, and yet they have hated both me and my Father. But this is to fulfill what is written in their Law: 'They hated me without reason.'"[16]

MIRACULOUS ACTS OF SERVICE

The miracles that Jesus performed were never capricious. They were always expressions of His love for people. Healing the sick, giving sight to the blind, calming the storm, casting out demons, and on three occasions, raising the dead[17]—these were clearly supernatural feats, identifying Him with God, and were done as expressions of His love. This was clear in His statement, "As the Father has loved me, so have I loved you."[18]

Jesus framed His own death as an act of service when he

said, "My command is this: Love each other as I have loved you. Greater love has no one than this, that he lay down his life for his friends." This love is further evidenced when Jesus said from the cross as He was dying, "Father, forgive them, for they do not know what they are doing."[19]

Paul the apostle clearly saw the death of Christ as an expression of God's love. Here are his words written to the church in Rome: "You see, at just the right time, when we were still powerless, Christ died for the ungodly. Very rarely will anyone die for a righteous man, though for a good man someone might possibly dare to die. But God demonstrates his own love for us in this: While we were still sinners, Christ died for us."[20]

Paul was overwhelmed with the thought that Christ would die, not for good people, but for sinners.

Earlier Jesus had prayed, "Father, I want those you have given me to be with me where I am, and to see my glory, the glory you have given me because you loved me before the creation of the world. I have made you known to them, and will continue to make you known in order that the love you have for me may be in them and that I myself may be in them."[21]

RESPONSES TO JESUS'
ACTS OF SERVICE

It is Jesus' identification with God the Father and His references of being with God before the world was created, as having come into the world from the Father, and His clear indications that He was returning to the Father after His death and resurrection, that have forced men who wish to be intellectually honest to conclude that there are only three possibilities.

Jesus is either a deliberate deceiver to be ignored, a deluded peasant to be pitied, or the divine Lord to be worshiped. There are no intellectual grounds for considering Him a great religious teacher. His claims of deity do not give us that option.

For all who examine the life of Jesus, He becomes a fork in the road of life. To those who choose the path of submission—who will bow the knee, submit the heart, and arise to walk humbly as His servants—many will testify that what ultimately won their hearts was His love expressed by miraculous acts of service and His sacrificial, voluntary death to pay the penalty for their sins.

6

GOD SPEAKS LOVE LANGUAGE #5: *Physical Touch*

A FEW YEARS AGO I WAS IN southern Germany to lead a marriage seminar one weekend and a parenting seminar the next. Karl was my interpreter for both events, and in all my travels I have never had a more enthusiastic interpreter.

With the first lecture, I could tell that this was going to be fun. As I entered into the personality of the characters in my stories, Karl joined me. When I crescendoed, he crescendoed. When I went into falsetto, Karl went into falsetto. When I moved my hands, he moved his hands. When I got intense, his eyes tightened as he followed me. When I broke into laughter, he laughed. In fact, at times I found myself laughing at him as he mimicked me.

About half of the audience understood English, so they laughed when I finished the story. The other half laughed when Karl finished the story. It was exciting!

During the breaks during both weekends, Karl served as my interpreter in personal conversations with those who were attending the seminars. We also had considerable time to talk with each other. Seven of my books had been translated into German. Karl was familiar with *The Five Love Languages* and was especially interested in my lecture on this book. He told me that his love language was definitely physical touch. Affectionate touches by his wife spoke deeply to him.

By the middle of the second seminar I was getting to know Karl pretty well. In one of our conversations he asked me, "What book are you writing now?" to which I responded, "I'm writing a book on the love languages of God. It is my hypothesis that people experience God's love more deeply when God speaks in their primary love language.

"For example," I continued, "if a person's primary love language is words of affirmation, they will experience God's love more deeply when it comes through words." I gave Karl the illustration of a young man who weeks earlier told me he came to God after stopping at a small hotel. Alienated from both parents and with little money, the traveler saw a Bible.

"In desperation I picked up a Gideon Bible," the traveler had told me. "It opened to Jeremiah chapter 31 and I read, 'I have loved you with an everlasting love; I have drawn you with loving-kindness.' And a few verses later, 'He who scattered Israel will gather them and will watch over his flock like a shepherd.'"

"I know the prophet was writing those words to Israel," the man said to me, "but that night they were God's words to me. I came back to God, and the next day returned home to my parents."

I explained to Karl that the power of God's words had spoken deeply to the traveler's spirit; God had spoken his primary love language.

A SLAP ON THE HAND

I noticed that Karl could hardly wait for me to finish my illustration. With great emotion he said, "That is certainly true of me. I told you last weekend that my primary love language is physical touch. Let me tell you how I came to be a Christian. I was seventeen years old and trying to decide what to believe about God. I wasn't sure there was a God, but if there was, I knew I wanted to know Him. I was riding my bicycle one night right after dark. I had a cigarette in my hand. I had been smoking since I was thirteen. I knew it wasn't good for me and I really wanted to quit. I had tried several times unsuccessfully. I looked down at my cigarette and said aloud, 'God, if You really exist, then take these cigarettes away from me.' Immediately, it was like a huge hand came out of nowhere, slapped my hand, and my cigarette was gone.

"I stopped my bicycle, and it was like the arms of God wrapped around me. I felt His presence. I wept. I knew that not only did God exist but that God loved me. From that day I have been a follower of Jesus. He spoke my love language."

"He touched me," Karl said, "and He still touches me. Not always, but often when I'm praying and singing, I can feel His presence. I know that God is a spirit, but when His Spirit touches my spirit, I feel it in my body. That is when I feel closest to God."

FEELING THE PRESENCE OF GOD

Karl's experience is not unusual. People whose primary love language is physical touch often speak of "feeling the presence of God." Remember Rod, whom we met in chapter 3? He was the husband of Greta, the speaker at the national women's conference. He was the one who made the God connection the second Sunday he attended a charismatic church. His friend had asked if he would like to go to the front of the church after the service and have people pray for him. Not wanting to offend his friend, he agreed.

Several men gathered around him and began to pray aloud. Rod said to me, "I had never experienced anything like it. Within a few minutes I was weeping uncontrollably and praying aloud myself, asking God to forgive me. God touched me that day. It was like electricity running through my body, and I felt totally clean."

Later in my conversation with Rod he said to me, "That was the beginning, but many times God has touched me since. Just two weeks ago, I was having a difficult time at work. Emotionally I was low. I was feeling disconnected from Greta. As I was driving down the road I said to God, 'I need You; I really need You.' I was overcome by the presence of God. It was like He was there with me in the car. I started weeping and had to pull off the road. I was overcome with joy and peace.

"His presence changed everything. I must have sat there fifteen minutes, weeping and praising God. When it was over I felt at peace. I knew that God was going to help me.

"I don't have those experiences with God very often," Rod continued. "I guess that's good. I'm not sure my body could handle it. But when it happens, it is sheer joy. Those are the highest moments in my life, when I know that I'm in the presence of God."

"What I hear you saying is that these deep physical, emotional experiences with God come only periodically," I replied. "Now, in the normal flow of life, when do you feel closest to God?"

>-•-<

"When I'm singing praise songs," Rod said, "I often feel God's presence. Sometimes when I'm at church, sometimes when I'm alone, it's like His presence passes by and I feel it like the wind. Sometimes I weep while I sing, but they are tears of joy. I know that God is there and I'm singing praise to Him."

THE EMBRACE OF A FATHER'S ARMS

As Rod told me about his experiences with God, my mind flashed to the island nation of Singapore, where I had visited some months earlier. I remembered the Saturday night I sat in a worship service at which I had been invited to speak. The congregational singing was being led by a small group of "praise singers," young people who appeared to be teenagers. As they sang, several began to raise their hands and eyes toward heaven. Tears began to flow down their faces as they sang praises to God.

After the service, I asked one of the ministers who these young people were. "Oh," he said, "those are young people who have been saved off the streets. They love God intently and they love to sing His praises."

As he told me that, my clinical mind began to paint a picture. Here were young people who had never known the warm embrace of a father's arms, who for whatever reason had been abandoned by their mothers but were experiencing the touch of a heavenly Father who has revealed Himself as "a father to the fatherless." They identified with the Hebrew songwriter who wrote, "Though my father and mother forsake me, the LORD will receive me."[1]

Later, I recalled that not all of the young "praise singers" were weeping. Not all were raising their hands heavenward, though all were singing praise to God. Some gave no evidence of being physically moved, but I had no reason to doubt that their praise was sincere. I wondered what their love language was and how God captured their hearts. I was relatively sure that those who wept had experienced the love of God most deeply by a conscious awareness of the presence of the living God. He touched them, and they felt His warm embrace. Feeling deeply loved by God, they reciprocated with raised hands and flowing tears.

PHYSICAL TOUCH AND NICHOLAS'S HOUSE CHURCH

Some months later, I was back in America visiting an inner-city "house church." These were young followers of Jesus who had never been inside a traditional Christian church. They had grown up with a totally secular worldview. They were in their late teens and early twenties. Most of them had experienced sex, alcohol, and drugs from their early teenage years. Most also had grown up in foster homes. Later I discovered that over half of them had never known their fathers. Before coming to the "house church," they had slept in the city park or under bridges if the weather was inclement.

Finding Family

These were not teens and young adults who had rebelled against their parents. They were young people who didn't know their parents. Through the ministry of a "house church" they had become followers of Jesus. They had found family and deliverance from their addictions. They had discovered the truth expressed in Psalm 68:6: "God sets the lonely in families, he leads forth the prisoners with singing."

In this setting I met Nicholas, a young man whose height, facial features, and hair reminded me of my own son. He appeared somewhat older than the rest of the group. I decided to engage him in conversation. We hadn't talked very long before he began to open up.

"I spent the first eighteen years of my life living on the streets of Chicago," he said. "Then I moved west. I ended up here, where I have been for the last ten years. I was sleeping in the park and washing dishes at a restaurant when a friend invited me to a rave. What I didn't know at the time was that it was a Christian rave. All night long we danced to the music, but periodically members of the band would talk about their own spiritual journey.

"It took a while, but I began to realize that they were all talking about God. It was strange to me. I had never heard anyone talk about God unless they were cursing, but God seemed to have made a difference in these people's lives. About four o'clock in the morning one of them said, 'If you would like someone to pray with you, come over to this end of the building.' I had never had anyone pray for me, so I thought it might be a good experience. I worked my way to that side of the building. I was met by this guy and gal who put their hands on my shoulder and said, 'Would you like to pray?'

"'I don't know how to pray,' I said.

"'We'll pray for you,' they said. So I sat down in this chair."

"God Was Touching My Life"

"They got on their knees with their hands on my shoulders, and both of them prayed for me. At the time I didn't know what was happening to me. I thought I was going crazy. Now I know God was touching my life and changing me. I felt a presence that I've never felt before, and I saw Jesus standing in front of me saying, 'I love you. I've always loved you. I want you to be My child. I want you to be My son. I want you to follow Me.' I didn't know who He was, so I said, 'Who are You?' And He said, 'I'm Jesus. I'm God's Son. I came to earth and I took your rap, and I took the rap for all your failures. I know you don't have a family. I want to be your Brother, and God wants to be your Father. These people who are praying for you are working for Me. They love you too, and they'll help you. Listen to them.'"

Nicholas said he answered, "OK. I will." When he did, he felt a heavy load "lifted off my shoulders," and he began to cry and to say, "Thank You, Jesus; thank You, Jesus; thank You, Jesus."

The next morning Nicholas decided to live with the couple who had prayed with him and some other people in a "house church."

"At the time I just thought it was a religious group of some kind. I've been here three years now. They have been the best three years of my life. God has delivered me from drugs, and for the first time in my life I have a family. Jesus has changed my life, and if He can change my life, He can change anybody's life."

TOUCH, COMPASSION, AND FERVENT PRAYER

During the three days I spent with this "house church" group, I discovered that prayer was more than a ritual for them. The first night a young girl came in who was obviously pregnant and appeared to be delusional. The first response of the leaders of the group was, "Let's pray for her." Six or eight of the people who were in the house at the time gathered around her, each of them putting one hand upon her body and their other hand clasping a fellow pray-er. My hand was joined with Nicholas's. One by one they began to pray for her.

They prayed with a love and intensity that I've seldom seen in a traditional church. When one was praying, the others were saying, "Yes, Lord," "Amen," "Thank You, Jesus," and "Lord, have mercy."

When Nicholas began to pray, his hand, which I was holding, began to tremble. As he continued to pray, the shake became more pronounced. When the prayer time was over, they stood, hugged each other, and hugged the young lady. They expressed praise to God for answering their prayers.

Then they took the young lady to the kitchen and fed her a meal. Later that evening, when they discovered she had no place to go, they invited her to spend the night.

The next day, when Nicholas and I were on the street doing a "prayer walk" (this is the practice of walking down the street praying for the people one passes and for those who live and work in the buildings, sometimes praying aloud and sometimes praying silently), I told Nicholas that I had never prayed with anyone whose hands shook as they prayed. "Oh, really?" he said. "I know that when my hands start shaking, the Spirit is on me and God wants to do something good through my prayers."

"Do you think that everyone's hand shakes if the Spirit is on them?" I asked.

"No, but it's always been true with me. I don't know why. Maybe it is just God's way of letting me know He's with me."

During my last night at the "house church," they asked me to share my message on *The Five Love Languages*. Some of them had heard bits and pieces, and one of them had read my book. I focused on how understanding someone's primary love language will help you more effectively meet their emotional need for love. I thought it would be helpful to them as they ministered to young people who so desperately needed love.

I did not anticipate Nicholas's response. As soon as the lecture was over, he rushed over to me and said, "Now I know why my hand shakes when I pray. My love language is definitely physical touch. It's God's way of showing me that He loves me."

I put my arms around him, patted him on the back, and said, "He does indeed, and so do I." Tears came to his eyes and to mine.

GOD'S TOUCH
UPON PEOPLE LONG AGO

Wrestling with God

Evidence that God speaks the love language of physical touch is seen throughout the Old Testament and the New Testament. Genesis 32 records the account of Jacob on his way to being reconciled with Esau, the brother from whom he had been estranged many years. Realizing that he had mistreated his brother and not knowing his brother's attitude after all these years, Jacob prayed, and as he prayed he encountered a spiritual presence in the form of a man who began to wrestle with him.

Perceiving the stranger to be a messenger of God, Jacob held onto the man and pleaded for a blessing. The man, wanting to be released before morning, "touched the socket of

Jacob's hip so that his hip was wrenched as he wrestled with the man." Before the man departed a blessing was given, but Jacob saw this as an encounter with God as evidenced by his words, "I saw God face to face, and yet my life was spared." The next morning Jacob "was limping because of his hip."[2] This experience was a major turning point in Jacob's life. His limping indicates that this was not simply a dream. Jacob was indeed touched by God.

Glowing from God's Presence

Moses also encountered God in a way that affected his physical body. When he descended the mountain where God had given him the Ten Commandments, the Scriptures say "he was not aware that his face was radiant because he had spoken with the LORD." This radiance was observed by others as evidenced by the fact that Moses "put a veil over his face."[3]

JESUS' TOUCH WHILE ON EARTH

Touching and Holding Children

When we examine the life of Jesus, we see Him often speaking the love language of physical touch. The Gospel According to Mark records that as Jesus was teaching in the villages, "people were bringing little children to Jesus to have him touch them."[4] The twelve disciples whom Jesus had chosen rebuked the people, thinking that Jesus was too busy for children. But Jesus said, "I tell you the truth, anyone who will not receive the kingdom of God like a little child will never enter it."

Then Mark records, "He took the children in his arms, put his hands on them and blessed them."[5]

Clearly this was not an isolated event if the people were bringing their children to Jesus to be touched and blessed. He had apparently been doing this in each of the villages which He visited.

Touching and Healing

Often as He performed miracles, Jesus touched the people involved. When He healed the man who had been blind from birth, it is interesting that the man remembered exactly how Jesus did it. When asked "How were your eyes opened?" he replied, "The man they call Jesus made some mud and put it on my eyes. He told me to go to Siloam and wash. So I went and washed, and then I could see."[6]

Matthew records that on one occasion "a man with leprosy came and knelt before him and said, 'Lord, if you are willing, you can make me clean.' Jesus reached out his hand and touched the man. 'I am willing,' he said. 'Be clean!' Immediately he was cured of his leprosy." Later that day as He came into the village of Capernaum, Jesus discovered that Peter's mother-in-law was sick with fever. "He touched her hand and the fever left her, and she got up and began to wait on him."[7]

A few days later in another village, Jesus encountered two blind men who followed Him, calling out, "Have mercy on us, Son of David!" . . . He touched their eyes and said, 'According to your faith will it be done to you'; and their sight was restored."[8]

Jesus also expressed the love language of touch to the twelve disciples. While Peter, James, and John were on the mountain with Jesus, His appearance underwent a stunning transformation. Three of the Gospels record this event, commonly referred to as the Transfiguration. As Matthew recorded it,

> *His face shone like the sun, and his clothes became as white as the light. Just then there appeared before them Moses and Elijah, talking with Jesus.*
>
> *. . . A bright cloud enveloped them, and a voice from the cloud said, "This is my Son, whom I love; with him I am well pleased. Listen to him!"*
>
> *When the disciples heard this, they fell facedown to the ground, terrified. But Jesus came and touched them. "Get up," he said. "Don't be afraid." When they looked up, they saw no one except Jesus.*[9]

Washing Feet

One of the most profound experiences in which Jesus touched the Twelve is recorded by the apostle John. What makes this event so important is that John prefaced it with Jesus' intention,

> *Jesus knew that the time had come for him to leave this world and go to the Father. Having loved his own who were in the world, he now showed them the full extent of his love.*
>
> *The evening meal was being served, and the devil had already prompted Judas Iscariot, son of Simon, to betray Jesus. Jesus knew that the Father had put all things under his power, and that he had come from God and was returning to God; so he got up from the meal, took off his outer clothing, and wrapped a towel around his waist.*[10]

John then described Jesus' next action: He filled a basin with water and began to wash His disciples' feet. Then He dried each man's feet with the towel. Once He had finished, Jesus dressed once more and returned to His place. Then He explained His actions.

> *"Do you understand what I have done for you?" he asked them. "You call me 'Teacher' and 'Lord,' and rightly so, for that is what I am. Now that I, your Lord and Teacher, have washed your feet, you also should wash one another's feet. I have set you an example that you should do as I have done for you. . . . Now that you know these things, you will be blessed if you do them."*[11]

Speaking Two Love Languages

Here Jesus spoke two of the five love languages, acts of service and physical touch. It was common practice in Jesus' day that when guests came for a meal, their feet would be washed by the household servant. Jesus took the role of the servant and lovingly washed the feet of His disciples. No doubt the touch of His hands was refreshing and restoring.

The true followers of Jesus have been serving and touching in His name throughout the centuries. They agree with Mother Teresa's answer when someone said to her that they would not touch the leper for a million dollars: "Neither would I. If it were a case of money, I would not even do it for two million. On the other hand, I do it gladly for the love of God."[12]

>––◄

THE EARLY CHURCH AND
THE LANGUAGE OF PHYSICAL TOUCH

More Touching and Healing

The book of Acts in the New Testament is the history of what God did through those early believers as they continued the serving, touching, healing ministry of Jesus. Here is an example. One afternoon Peter and John were going up to the temple to pray. They encountered a man at the temple gate who had been crippled from birth. As they were about to go in the gate, he asked them for money. Peter's answer was:

"Silver or gold I do not have, but what I have I give you. In the name of Jesus Christ of Nazareth, walk." Taking him by the right hand, he helped him up, and instantly the man's feet and ankles became strong. He jumped to his feet and began to walk. Then he went with them into the temple courts, walking and jumping, and praising God. When all the people saw him walking and praising God, they recognized him as the same man who used to sit begging at the temple gate called Beautiful, and they were filled with wonder and amazement at what had happened to him.[13]

The lame man, having been touched by God through the hands of Peter and John, reciprocated his love by hugging Peter and John. The astonished crowd assembled, and Peter said, "Men of Israel, why does this surprise you? Why do you stare at us as if by our own power or godliness we have made this man walk? The God of Abraham, Isaac and Jacob, the God of our fathers, has glorified his servant Jesus." Peter then described the death of "the Holy and Righteous One" and explained that "God raised him from the dead." Then Peter added, "By faith in the name of Jesus, this man whom you see and know was made strong. It is Jesus' name and the faith that comes through him that has given this complete healing to him, as you can all see."[14]

Touching That Makes the God Connection

Such healing touches, both by Jesus and His followers, did not end with the physical healing. The physical miracle was to validate Jesus' claims and bring men to respond to His love and establish an eternal relationship with God. This is evidenced by what Peter said after the crippled man was healed. Noting how they had agreed to the death of Jesus, Peter explained that Jesus' death fulfilled the prophets' words that "[God's] Christ would suffer." Then Peter urged his listeners, "Repent . . . and turn to God, so that your sins may be wiped out, that times of refreshing may come from the Lord, and that he may send the Christ, who has been appointed for you—even Jesus. He must remain in heaven until the time comes for God to restore everything."[15]

Peter was calling them to respond to the love of God. The touch of God, which brought healing to the blind, caused crippled men to walk, and delivered Nicholas from drug addiction, is always for the purpose of helping people make the God connection.

Blinding—and Healing—a Skeptic

In the first century and today, some are skeptical of those who claim to be "touched by God." But the greatest skeptics become the greatest believers when they themselves are touched by God. Saul of Tarsus is an example. He was a first-century zealot intent on stamping out what he considered to be a heretical sect that claimed that Jesus of Nazareth was the Messiah. He was on his way to the town of Damascus with legal papers in his pouch to arrest and return to Jerusalem anyone who was teaching this heresy.

But as he neared Damascus, a bright light from heaven flashed around him. The dazed zealot fell to the ground. The book of Acts describes what happened next.

> [He] heard a voice say to him, "Saul, Saul, why do you persecute me?"
>
> "Who are you, Lord?" Saul asked.
>
> "I am Jesus, whom you are persecuting," he replied. "Now get up and go into the city, and you will be told what you must do."
>
> The men traveling with Saul stood there speechless; they heard the sound but did not see anyone. Saul got up from the ground, but when he opened his eyes he could see nothing. So they led him by the hand into Damascus. For three days he was blind, and did not eat or drink anything."[16]

Clearly Saul had been touched by God. At the end of three days, God sent a man named Ananias to the house where Saul was staying. "Ananias went to the house and entered it." Significantly, he placed his hands on Saul. Then he said, "'Brother Saul, the Lord—Jesus, who appeared to you on the road as you were coming here—has sent me so that you may see again and be filled with the Holy Spirit.' Immediately, something like scales fell from Saul's eyes, and he could see again. He got up and was baptized, and after taking some food, he regained his strength."[17]

Saul's life was never the same. He spent several days with the believers in Damascus and soon "began to preach in the synagogues that Jesus is the Son of God. All those who heard him were astonished and asked, 'Isn't he the man who raised havoc in Jerusalem among those who call on this name?' . . . Saul grew more and more powerful and baffled the Jews living in Damascus by proving that Jesus is the Christ."[18]

Saul (who would become the apostle Paul) spent the rest of his life seeking to convince Jews and Gentiles that Jesus was indeed the Son of God. Read the book of Acts in the New Testament and you will see him beaten, imprisoned, and often threatened by death, but nothing dampened the spirit of this man who had been touched by God.

Since the first century, thousands of men and women have claimed to have been touched by God. They, in turn, have touched others as representatives of Christ. They work in hospitals, giving baths and wiping fevered brows. You will find them in rescue missions, kneeling beside the homeless with an arm draped around the shoulder of a needy person. They serve as "greeters" in their churches. These are the people who, with a smile, extend a hand and give an affirming "pat on the back" as people enter the house of worship. They are channels of God's love, speaking fluently the love language of physical touch.

7

><

DISCOVERING
YOUR PRIMARY
LOVE LANGUAGE

$\mathcal{H}$OW DO I LOVE THEE? Let me count the ways."
When Elizabeth Barrett Browning asked and answered this
question in her *Sonnet 42,* she implied that the ways of expressing love are limited only by man's ability to be creative.
Of course, Browning was right, and when a man and woman
are in the obsessive state of the "in love" experience, they
can be extremely creative.

Rhonda, a farmer's wife, once told me about her husband's
invitation to take the afternoon off and go flying with him.
She knew he was not a pilot and asked, "What do you mean?"

"Jim and I were flying the other day, and I saw something that I want you to see." Being adventuresome by nature,
she agreed.

Once they had circled the county, they returned to fly

over their farm. Jim tilted the plane and her husband pointed to the wheat fields below in which she read clearly the words, "I love you, Rhonda." Months earlier, her husband had carefully double-seeded these letters, knowing that once the wheat had sprouted, the words could be seen from the sky. Yes, man is creative, and there are thousands of ways to express love.

PREDICTABLE WAYS
WE SAY, "I LOVE YOU"

However, in the course of daily life most of us are not as creative. Our expressions of love tend to fall into predictable patterns, and these patterns are greatly influenced by our own primary love language. Remember, of the five love languages, one language speaks to each of us more deeply than the other four; this is our primary love language. So if you are married and your husband's primary love language is words of affirmation, speak this language often, and his love tank will be full and he will feel secure in your love. If your primary love language is acts of service, and your husband speaks this language regularly, your love tank will be full and you will feel secure in his love. If, however, your husband fails to speak the love language acts of service and you fail to speak words of affirmation, neither of you will have a full love tank, even though some of the other four languages are spoken.

That is why couples can be sincerely loving each other but not connecting emotionally. The problem is not their sincerity; the problem is they are not speaking each other's primary love language.

If we simply do what comes naturally for us, we will tend to speak our own love language. If my primary love language is words of affirmation, then I will tend to use words to express my love for my wife. I am giving her what would make me feel extremely loved. But if that is not her primary love language, words will not mean to her what they would mean to me. Most of my creativity will be used in exploring various ways to verbally express my love to her. I may write love notes and leave them in unexpected places. I may request the local deejay to play her favorite love song on the radio. I may even write the words "I love you" in a wheat field, but my efforts at expressing love will tend to focus on using words of affirmation. On the other hand, if my wife's love language is acts of service, she may discover a dozen ways to serve me, all of which she views as deep expressions of love.

THE GOD WHO SHAKES HANDS WITH YOU

The same tendency is true when it comes to receiving and reciprocating God's love. Theoretically I may agree that God speaks His love to me in a thousand ways, but experientially I feel more deeply loved when I sense that God is speaking my primary love language.

A few weeks ago I walked into my office on Monday morning and found that my secretary had placed a photocopy of a note that had been placed in the offering plate of our church the day before. It said simply this:

> To:
> The church who shakes
> hands with me.
> From:
> Michael Curlee
> Age: 5

No mention of the songs, sermon, offering plates, drama, or stained glass windows. What church means to Michael is "someone shakes my hand." Michael's primary love language is physical touch. I don't know if Michael has made the connection between God and God's helpers who attend his church, but I predict that eventually he will. Someday God will shake Michael's hand and embrace him, and Michael will make the God connection.

RETURNING GOD'S LOVE
IN OUR LANGUAGE

Conversely, when we reciprocate God's love, we tend to express our love in our primary love language. I first met Floyd in Houston. He was operating the sound system for a national convention of pro athletes. I had given my lecture on *The Five Love Languages* the day before. During one of our breaks, Floyd stopped me and said, "Your lecture on *The Five Love Languages* has helped me understand my marriage. My love language is physical touch, and my wife's love language is acts of service. To be honest, we are not doing very well in speaking each other's language. Actually, I never understood this before. I knew she complained that I didn't help her around the house. I also knew that she would often draw back when I tried to kiss or hug her. Now I understand; both of us have empty love tanks.

"I can't wait to get home and shock my wife by washing dishes and vacuuming the floors and making beds. Do you think if I start speaking her language, she will start speaking mine?"

"I can't guarantee that," I said, "but I can tell you that's the best thing you can do to improve your marriage. If your wife begins to see you speaking her primary love language, there is a good possibility that she will begin to have warm emotional feelings for you and eventually will begin to reciprocate love."

Later, I had a more extended conversation with Floyd in which we discussed spiritual matters. I discovered that Floyd had become a follower of Jesus about three years earlier and had become very active in a contemporary church. "I never cared much for God," he said, "and the church always turned me off. But a friend invited me to this new church. It was different from anything I've ever seen. The place was wired. I felt God the first night I went there. The second time I went, I found myself overwhelmed by the presence of God. I was at the front of the church, weeping at the altar, before I knew what happened. That's the night I asked God to come into my life and forgive me of my past. It was the greatest night of my life."

As I talked with Floyd about what had happened since that night, eventually I asked him, "How do you express your love to God?"

"What I like is the praise music. I just reach out and touch God when I'm singing. I get goose bumps," he answered. "That's what moves me. It's like God is all over the place, and I am caught up in worshiping Him."

"It sounds like your love language toward God is also physical touch," I said.

Floyd was silent for a moment, then a smile broke across his face. "I've never thought of it that way, but you're right. It's when my emotions are moved and I feel the presence of God that my love tank fills up and I could worship God forever."

Floyd was confirming what I was coming to believe, that

an individual's method of worship or method of expressing love to God is strongly influenced by his or her primary love language. We can learn to speak other love languages, and we should; I'll discuss that later. But the most natural way for you to experience and express love toward God is by speaking your primary love language.

THREE KEY QUESTIONS

How then do we discover our primary love language? In human relationships, I have often suggested the following approach. Ask yourself three questions. First, *How do I most often express love to other people?* If you regularly express words of appreciation, affirmation, and love to others, there is a good chance that your primary love language is words of affirmation. You are giving to others what you would like to receive yourself. If you are often patting other people on the back or touching them on the shoulder, or giving appropriate hugs, then your primary love language may be physical touch.

Second, ask yourself, *What do I complain about most often?* Your complaints reveal your inner emotional need for love. The wife who says, "We don't ever spend time together anymore," is revealing that quality time is her primary love language. The husband who says, "I just feel like you don't love me anymore. If I didn't initiate kissing you, I don't think you would ever kiss me." His complaints are revealing that his primary love language is physical touch. The child who complains "You mean you didn't bring me anything from your trip?" is telling you that gifts is her primary love language.

Third, ask yourself, *What do I request most often?* The wife who says "Could we take a walk this evening after dinner?" is requesting quality time. If she often makes such requests, she is revealing that her primary love language is quality time. We tend to request from others what would meet our deepest emotional need for love.

If you will answer those three questions, you will likely discover your primary love language in human relationships.

THREE QUESTIONS ABOUT YOUR RELATIONSHIP WITH GOD

Once you discover your primary love language in human relationships, you can assume that this is also your primary love language in your relationship with God. However, if you want to check it out, you can ask and answer the same three questions. First, *How do I most often express my love to God?* If, upon reflection, you find that you are the kind of person who volunteers when the Bible study leader asks, "Who could make a meal to take to the Brown family?" you are demonstrating that acts of service is your primary love language. You genuinely feel that when you are serving others you are serving God, thus you express your love by acts of service. You are also deeply moved when you read the life of Jesus and see Him healing the sick, feeding the hungry, and washing the feet of His disciples. It is the serving nature of Christ that grips you most deeply and draws you to God.

Your neighbor's answer to that question may be altogether different. She may say, "I feel closest to God and feel that I am honoring Him most by my daily quiet time with Him. Every morning I get up early so we can spend time together. It's the highlight of my day. I sense that God is talking to me as I read the Scriptures, and I talk to Him as I pray. It's like a daily conversation with God. It's the same thing I like to do with my husband when he comes home from work in the evenings." Quality time is your neighbor's primary love language.

The second question can also be very revealing: *What do I most often complain to God about?* Suppose you complain, "God, I just feel like You've abandoned me. I don't feel close to You. I used to read Your Word and weep. Now I'm just reading words on a page. At church I used to feel Your presence when we sang, but now it seems like I'm just going through the motions. What's wrong?" This complaint is likely revealing that your primary love language is physical touch. It is what Floyd called the "manifest presence of God." He sensed that God touched him, not only spiritually but in the body; he felt God's presence.

This "touch" may be revealed by tears or even by chill bumps or shaking. It is through this spiritual, physical experience that Floyd was keenly aware of God's love, and it is in these experiences that he expresses his love to God.

On the other hand, perhaps you complain, "Lord, it just seems like You're not blessing me anymore. For a while, every time I turned around You were blessing me. Now, I can hardly pay the bills. It looks like I am going to lose my job, and now our baby is sick. I don't understand." If that's your complaint, your primary love language probably is receiving gifts. When the gifts of job, money, and health were being received, you felt loved by God. Now that those are no longer present, you feel that God doesn't love you.

What about the person who complains that the pastor's sermons are rambling and meaningless? That person's primary love language probably is words of affirmation. Because he or she is not hearing anything meaningful from the pastor, the individual does not feel God's love through the sermon. Our complaints often reveal our primary love language.

The third question, *What do I request of God most often?* may also confirm your primary love language. Listen to the prayers you pray, especially the requests you make while praying, and you may discover your primary love language. Bob prays most often for wisdom and acknowledges that his primary love language is words of affirmation. "As I read the wisdom literature of the Old Testament, particularly the book of Proverbs, I feel that I am walking close to the heart of God. Whenever the Holy Spirit shows me how to apply the wisdom of the Bible in my personal life, I feel that God is giving me personal attention, and I feel deeply loved and grateful."

Mary prays most often for the health of her children and that God will meet the financial needs of the family. She recognizes that receiving gifts is her primary love language. When God answers her prayers, she feels extremely loved by God.

Randall's most common prayer is, "Lord, I want to feel Your presence. I want to know Your power. I want to feel Your hand upon me. I want to be anointed by Your Spirit." When God answers his prayer, and he experiences God's presence in a way that affects him physically and emotionally, he senses the love of God deeply and reciprocates with raised hands and flowing tears, and has even been known to dance in the presence of God. His love language is physical touch.

Doris's primary love language is quality time, and her most common prayer is, "Lord, help me to find time to be alone with You. My life is so filled with activity and responsibilities. More than anything, I want to spend time with You. Help me to find time." Her sister, Janice, has a much different prayer. "Lord, help me to find time to work in the soup kitchen. You know how much that means to me. You know how much I want to serve others in Your name. Help me to find time to do the ministry that is on my heart." Her primary love language is acts of service.

Most people will be able to identify their primary love language by answering the above three questions. Most people will also discover that their primary love language remains the same in both human relationships and their relationship with God.

HOW KNOWING YOUR LOVE LANGUAGE AFFECTS YOUR RELATIONSHIP WITH GOD AND OTHERS

The logical question is "How does understanding my primary love language affect my relationship with God and others?" Let me suggest the following ways.

1. Better Self-understanding

If I know my primary love language, it gives me greater self-understanding. "I now know why my daily quiet time with God is so important to me," said one man I'll call Dave. "My love language is quality time. Nothing is more important in my life than the thirty minutes I spend with God every morning.

"I hear other people say that having a daily devotional time requires so much discipline on their part. That has never been true for me," Dave continued. "It takes almost no discipline. It means more to me than eating breakfast. It is where I find my strength for the day. For me, it's a privilege to spend time listening to God and sharing my own thoughts and feelings with Him. It is what keeps my relationship with God alive."

Why is it so easy for him and so difficult for many others

to maintain consistency in a daily quiet time with God? Because quality time is his primary love language. For him, this is the most natural and meaningful way of receiving and reciprocating the love of God.

Beth is a twenty-five-year-old single mother. After participating in a workshop on *The Love Languages of God,* she said, "Now I understand why reading devotional books is so important to me. My love language is words of affirmation. Almost every morning when I read the comments of the writer, I find a sentence or an idea that speaks deeply to me and gives me the encouragement and strength and love to go on with my responsibilities. The words are like food to my soul. That's also why I have three or four musical tapes that I play constantly in my car as I drive to work. When I hear "He's my Rock and my Salvation; whom shall I fear?" I feel like I can conquer the world. I know that God is with me. It is the words of those songs that give me the assurance that God loves me."

Later in our conversation, Beth said, "Now I also understand why singing worship songs to God is so important to me. I feel like the words express my heart of gratitude and love to God more than anything else."

I met Roger at a church in Singapore. He was enthusiastic about his faith and his weekly prayer meeting with other men. "At our church on Sunday mornings, we have a prayer meeting before the service. A small group of men get together to pray for each other and to pray for the service. One man gets on his knees while the other men lay their hands on his shoulders and pray for him. When the men lay their hands on my shoulders and begin praying for me, it's like God has put His hand on my shoulders. It's the highlight of my week. I never feel closer to God than when those men are praying for me. It's like electricity runs through my body as they pray. I'm prepared not only for the service, but I'm prepared to live another week loving God.

"I understand now why that is so important to me," Roger explained. "My love language is physical touch. Through those men, the Lord is touching me, and I feel His presence. Once in a while I have to miss the morning service because of my work, but I would do anything not to miss that prayer meeting."

Someone else might find such a prayer meeting uncomfortable. To attend such a meeting regularly could become burdensome, but not for Roger. Physical touch is his primary love language, and this is where he feels the touch of God. If you know your primary love language, you then understand why certain aspects of your relationship with God seem natural and speak so deeply to your soul.

2. Better Able to Understand and Help Fellow Pilgrims

There is also a second benefit. If you know your primary love language, you will better understand those fellow pilgrims who are different from you. Roger made this truth perfectly clear later during our conversation. He explained that his wife was critical of his wanting to attend that early morning prayer meeting. "She didn't understand how important it was to me until we discussed the love language concept. I must confess it also helped me understand her. In my heart, I was always critical of her because she didn't attend the women's prayer meeting. I thought if she really loved God she would want to go to that meeting. After reading your book, I discovered that my wife's primary love language is quality time. She spends forty-five minutes every day in prayer and meditation over the Scriptures. I always admired her for that. When our pastor challenged us to have an extended time with God every day, I always felt guilty because I knew my wife was much better at that than I. Now I understand why it has been so hard for me and so easy for her. Quality time is her primary love language. The love she receives and gives to God in her daily time with Him is what I receive on Sunday mornings when God touches me.

"Now I understand that both are valid ways of receiving God's love and expressing love to God. My wife is no longer critical about my attending the prayer meeting. She now understands how important it is to me and my relationship with God."

Clearly, knowing someone's love language can help you understand that person's walk with God. And it's especially helpful in understanding a spouse's relationship with God. Madeline was a cheerful woman whom I judged to be in her early fifties (though I know it is always dangerous to guess a woman's age). She said to me, "I want to thank you for helping me understand my husband. For years I complained about how much money he gives away. He gives to everybody who asks for money, even the men who are holding the hunger signs at the traffic light.

"I used to tell him, 'You're just giving them money to get drunk.' He would say, 'But maybe they're hungry.' He probably gives to seventy-five Christian organizations around the world. I don't mean just once; I mean every month. Our checkbook looks like a religious roster.

"Once I said to him, 'If giving gets you to heaven, then you're going to have a mansion,' to which he replied, 'You don't get to heaven by giving. You get to heaven by accepting God's gift of eternal life through Jesus Christ. I'm not giving to get to heaven,' he said. 'I'm giving because I'm going to heaven, and I want to show people the love of God on my way.'

"In my heart I knew he was right, but it always seemed to me that he was overdoing it. Now that I've heard about the five love languages, I understand my husband. Giving gifts is his primary love language. He is hopelessly in love with Jesus. His greatest joy is in giving to the causes of Christ around the world."

"Does he also give gifts to you?" I inquired.

"Oh, all the time!" she said. "I've never had any complaints about that, though sometimes I've felt he overdid that also. Now I just accept them and say thank you."

Later I inquired of Madeline, "So, do you give gifts to him as well?"

"Interesting that you should ask," she said. "After we read and discussed your book, I said to him, 'But I have not given you many gifts through the years. Have you really felt my love?' His response was, "Oh, Madeline, you have given me the gift of your presence, the gift of your commitment, the gift of your beauty, the gift of three children, the gift of hundreds of meals, the gift of encouragement.' He went on and on. To him everything is a gift."

"My guess is that your primary love language is not gifts," I continued. "Am I correct?"

"You're right," she said. "My love language is words of affirmation. And since we read the book he's become much better at speaking my language. Before, he thought gifts were the answer to everything. Now he understands that we are different. He's always given me a fair amount of verbal affirmation, but now he's becoming proficient in speaking my language. However, the biggest difference is that I'm no longer complaining about all that he gives away. I know that it is his way of loving God, and I am fortunate to be married to such a man." Madeline's attitude changed when she understood her husband's primary love language.

THOSE LOVE LANGUAGES IN ACTION

On the Blue Ridge Highway

A few years ago, my wife and I were traveling on the Blue Ridge Parkway in the mountains of North Carolina. We had stopped at one of the shops featuring mountain crafts. I walked through the store with her and then wandered outside as she continued browsing. On the porch of the shop were rockers. I sat down and began to rock. The man beside me was friendly and began talking almost immediately. When he found out that I did counseling at a church, he said, "I want to ask you a question. I've got a brother-in-law who goes to one of these holy roller churches. What do you think of those kinds of churches? Is that stuff real?"

Not wanting to answer before I fully understood the question, I inquired, "What kind of holy roller church is this?"

"Well, they say it is a Baptist church, but it's not like any Baptist church I've ever seen."

"Have you visited the church with your brother-in-law?" I asked.

"Once," he said, "and I swore I would never go back."

I asked him to describe it.

"Well, they sing these gospel songs and everybody gets happy and shouts. I mean, they run up and down the aisles. They say, 'Hallelujah, praise the Lord.' One lady was waving a white handkerchief and crying, saying, 'Thank You, Jesus!

Thank You, Jesus!' My brother-in-law raised both hands and danced in the aisle. It was like he was in a trance or something. It was like nothing I've ever seen."

"Have you talked with your brother-in-law about his religious beliefs?" I asked.

"Yes," he said. "Actually, we agree on almost everything. He believes in the Bible; he believes Jesus is the Son of God and that we get to heaven by trusting in Jesus' death and resurrection. I'm a Baptist too, and we believe the same thing. It's just that his worship style is so different from mine. To me, it's just too much emotion. I don't understand it."

By this time my wife had come out of the shop, and I knew she wasn't interested in listening to me talk to a stranger for an hour about religion, so I said to him, "I think I understand your brother-in-law but I don't have time to explain it." I went to my car and got a copy of my book *The Five Love Languages,* took it back to the man and said, "Here's a book I wrote. It's not on the subject of religion. It's on the subject of marriage, but if you will read this book I think it will help you understand your brother-in-law."

I gave him my card and said, "After you've read the book, call me and we will discuss it further." He expressed appreciation for the book, then Karolyn and I continued our afternoon of escape from the city.

Horace and His Wife

It was probably six months later when my secretary said to me, "There's a man by the name of Horace on the phone; says he met you on the Blue Ridge Parkway." I didn't remember that he ever gave me his name, but I remembered the man I had met on the Blue Ridge Parkway, so I took the call. He began, "Do you remember our conversation on the Blue Ridge Parkway about my brother-in-law and his holy roller church?"

"I certainly do."

"Well, my wife and I read your book. How did you know that we were having trouble in our marriage?"

I laughed and said, "Well, I didn't know that, but I thought the book might help you understand your brother-in-law."

"It did that, but it also helped our marriage. I don't read many books," he said, "but this book was easy to read and it made a lot of sense. My wife and I discussed it, and we are learning to speak each other's primary love language. It has really helped our marriage!"

Horace and His Brother-in-Law

"Well, I'm glad. How about your brother-in-law? Did it give you any insight into him?"

"Well, the first thing I did after my wife finished reading the book was give it to my brother-in-law and his wife. They read it in a few weeks and discussed it with each other, and one night we had dinner together. He told us that his love language was physical touch and his wife's love language was acts of service. They had also been having some struggles in their marriage, and the book really helped them. I didn't make the connection right away, but the next week I was thinking about our conversation and why you would have given me a book on marriage when I was asking you a question about religion. Then it hit me. My brother-in-law's love language was physical touch, so his method of worship was physical.

"It was like a light came on, and I said to myself, 'That makes a lot of sense. His worship of God is physical because physical touch is his primary love language. He is really loving God when he raises his hands and dances in the aisle.'

"A couple of weeks later my brother-in-law and I were hunting and I brought up the subject. He had not made the connection. But when I shared my thoughts with him, he said, 'You know, Horace, that makes a lot of sense. My wife has never gotten into worship like I do. She's more of the quiet type. Maybe this explains why. I always felt she was not as spiritual as I was because she did not get into worship like I did. Her love language is acts of service, and now that we are talking about this I realize that she is always doing things for people. She fixes meals when somebody in the church is sick. When there is a death in the community, she goes over and helps clean the house for the family, and of course takes food. She's always doing something for people. She visits in the nursing homes every week.'"

Horace's brother-in-law then added, "Now I'm beginning to see this is her way of showing her love for God. She's speaking her love language. Man, I'm glad we talked about this, Horace. I would never have thought about this if we hadn't had this conversation."

Horace's Book Idea

Horace concluded his "what happened after you left" account with the final outcome and a suggestion. "So now I understand my brother-in-law and he understands his wife. Maybe you ought to write a book on the love languages of God. It might help a lot of people understand others better."

"Maybe I should," I said. "I'll give some thought to that."

As the reader now knows, I did give it some thought and

I did write the book. I hope that many others will experience the insight that Horace experienced.

While He was on earth, Jesus of Nazareth prayed that those who became His followers would see themselves in unity, not only with Him and His Father, but with each other. In my opinion, one of the tragedies of the last two thousand years is that the followers of Jesus have been too often critical of each other. Some of these criticisms have focused on "methods of worship." Let us recognize that the human heart has indeed many languages of love with which to worship God.

8

>—<

LEARNING TO SPEAK
NEW DIALECTS OF LOVE

*W*E ARE CREATURES OF HABIT. From the time we rise in the morning, we tend to go through the same routines day after day. Think about it. How different was this morning from yesterday morning? Chances are as you made your way from the bed to the bathroom you began to approach your day much as you have approached every day for months. The soap, the toothbrush, the washcloth, the toilet—they all have their place and typically stay in order.

Now, there is nothing wrong with order. In fact, doing the same things in the same order may even conserve time. But repetition may also foster dullness and, eventually, boredom.

We are also innately creative. As we tap into our creative nature, life becomes more exciting and less predictable. For a number of years I have purposely chosen to vary my morning routine at least one morning a week simply for the sake of variety. Perhaps it is breakfast before shaving, rather than after shaving. Perhaps it is breakfast in suit and tie, rather than my flannel pajamas draped over a V-neck T shirt. I may even break my grapefruit-Cheerios routine and do something really radical, like white grape juice and Frosted Flakes. What about the eggs and sausage, grits and sawmill gravy? Oh, I even do that once a year!

Variety stimulates the mind. It is easier to keep the mind active if you change the routine. I have enjoyed this bit of morning creativity so much that I have even begun to work it into the rest of my day. Nothing breaks the dullness of the afternoon like a twenty-minute drive to the other side of town, savoring two Krispy Kreme doughnuts—with skim milk, of course. After such an outing, I can walk back into the office feeling like I have been on an adventure. A growing number of employees are learning the value of these mini-vacations in the middle of the workday. Creativity livens up what could be a life of monotonous routine.

EXPRESSING LOVE TO GOD
IN NEW WAYS

I would like to suggest that the same principle applies to our love relationship with God. If we simply do what comes naturally and express our love to God in our usual manner, it is possible that even our relationship with God will become routine. Once while visiting England with my college-aged son, we spent an afternoon in Salisbury Cathedral. Part of the time we walked together, but a good bit of the time we went solo, lingering before stained glassed windows, sitting and observing sincere worshipers, marveling at the architectural style, even ascending the stairs and viewing the other side of the vaulted ceilings of the cathedral.

As the sun began to set, Derek and I settled into the grass of the beautiful lawn surrounding the cathedral. Looking toward the cathedral, I said to him, "Would you like to pray?"

To which Derek responded, "Dad, I have been praying for two hours."

A New Dialect of Prayer

I was silenced by his answer. Now, don't misunderstand me; I was deeply moved by my cathedral experience. In fact, that is why I invited him to pray. I wanted us to share the afterglow of the experience. But I must be honest. It never occurred to me to pray as I walked through the cathedral. I was too absorbed in structure and form.

Later, as I reflected upon that experience, I realized that I had managed to limit prayer to certain routine boundaries which I had established: sitting down, or kneeling, closing my eyes and talking to God. My son had discovered a new dialect of prayer, one that involved walking, not only with an open heart but with open eyes. He taught me a dialect I have enjoyed ever since. Now, it does not even take a cathedral. I often pray aloud as I drive down the freeway (with my eyes open, of course).

Speaking New Dialects and Other Languages

Each of the five love languages has many dialects, but many of us have limited ourselves to the few with which we have become accustomed. In this chapter, I want to explore the possibility of enhancing your love relationship with God by learning to speak new dialects of your primary love language, or you may be really creative and try speaking a totally different love language, perhaps one you've never spoken before. If God is not limited in the love languages and dialects He speaks, we need not be, either. In true worship, we can honor our Creator in many ways.

We will look at each of the five love languages, and I will give brief accounts of various dialects of speaking this language to God. These are only representative, of course. With a little creativity, you may discover a dialect that has never crossed your mind and, in so doing, bring a new dimension to your relationship with God. Let's begin with words of affirmation.

SPEAKING WORDS OF AFFIRMATION

One of the dialects of words of affirmation is *thanksgiving.* One of my favorite psalms is Psalm 100. Perhaps it is my favorite because I memorized it as a child. In that psalm David wrote, "Enter his gates with thanksgiving" (verse 4). Thanksgiving is one of the best-known dialects of words of affirmation. But even here, we tend to limit ourselves to certain expressions of thanks over and over again. "Thank You for my spouse and children. Thank You for our food. Thank You for life and health." These and similar expressions, if repeated often enough, may become simply routine and may even be spoken without consciously thinking of what we are saying.

Giving Thanks for *All* Things

Several years ago I was challenged to think more creatively about expressions of thanksgiving to God. Her name was

Emily, and she was attending a conference where I was speaking. I don't remember how the subject of thanksgiving worked its way into the conversation, but I do remember what she said. "Let me tell you what a wonderful experience I had this week. You know how so much of our praying involves asking God for things? Well, I decided on Wednesday morning that I was not going to ask God for anything, but I was going to thank Him for the things He had already given me.

"I looked around my house and realized that it was filled with things that made my life easier and things which brought back memories. So I determined to thank God for each of them."

Then Emily described for me how she did that. "I lay on my bed and thanked Him for the bed, mentioning the pillow, the mattress, the sheet, the blanket, and the beautifully decorated bedspread. I put my hand on the telephone and thanked Him for the phone and that it was cordless, so I could walk around the house while I talked. I thanked Him for the nightstand on which the phone was sitting and for the drawer which gave me a place to hide my neck brace. I touched the shade of the lamp that was sitting on the nightstand and thanked Him for giving Thomas Edison such a wonderful idea and for letting me have a lamp by which to read as I went to bed at night.

"I walked to the window, touched the blinds, and thanked Him that with a pull of one string I could have privacy. I touched the drapes and thanked Him that, not only did they match the spread, but several years earlier He had given me the ability to make them—which took my mind to the electric sewing machine. So I walked into the sewing room and thanked Him for the machine. While there, I thanked Him for the table on which I could stretch my fabric, for a yardstick, for patterns, and for a beautifully lighted room which stimulated my creative spirit.

"I walked to the bathroom, turned on the faucet, put my hand under the water, and thanked Him that I had running water. I touched the hot and cold faucets and thanked Him that I had a choice. I sat down on the commode and thanked Him that I did not have to walk a path to an outhouse like the one I had seen on my Uncle George's farm. I stepped into the shower and thanked Him that I didn't have to go to the river to take a bath. I thanked Him for the rugs that kept my feet from touching the cold tile floor, for the thick white towel that I wrapped around my body. When I looked at all the creams, oils, and tools sitting around my sink, I thanked Him not only for their presence, but for that voice within me that said as I looked in the mirror, 'Be creative; you can look better than that!'

"Later I sat in my chair in the den and thanked Him— not only for that chair but for all the chairs in my house. I walked through the room, touching every object. I touched the picture of my grandmother and thanked God for the reminder that I have a godly heritage. I touched the clock given to me by my grandfather just before he died and thanked God for the memory of him. I touched the two candles and thanked Him for a backup the next time the thunderstorm knocked out the electricity. I touched the books laying on the floor beside my chair and thanked Him for the many people who have enriched my life by their writings.

"For one hour," she said, "I walked through my house thanking God for the things He had given me. I still have four more rooms to go. I am going to have another hour of thanksgiving next week."

Giving Thanks for People

I have never forgotten my conversation with Emily. She enriched my life forever. Since then, I have had my own thanksgiving hours, touching most of the objects in my own house and verbalizing thanksgiving to God. Of course, thanking God for material objects is but one small arena of thanksgiving. Many meaningful hours could be spent in thanking God for the people He has brought into your life.

Try it sometime. You will be astounded at the number of people for whom you can give thanks. Start with your immediate family; then go to your extended family. (You may find yourself wanting to say about certain family members, "Thank You for this person, but I wish You would have made them with a little more kindness." Don't yield to this temptation. Think of something good that they have done or said and give God thanks.)

When you have walked through your extended family, think about the persons who have taught you in school and in church. Dust off your school annuals and look through the pictures of your classmates, and thank God for all those whom you knew. Think about the people in your neighborhood who have done kind deeds through the years, friends in your Bible study group who continue to impact your life in a positive way, the people who stock the grocery shelves where you shop, the firemen and policemen who protect your city, the sanitary engineer who collects your garbage each week; and don't forget the people who have influenced your spiritual development through the years.

Giving Thanks for Much, Much More

Then there is the natural world around you: grass and trees, flowers and butterflies, fleecy clouds and the winds that move them, raindrops on roses and sunshine on daisies, mountains and plains, beaches and rivers. Then you can visit the zoo and start your litany of thanksgiving for the world of animals.

Pull out the encyclopedia and look up the article on the human body. Thank Him for your thyroid gland, sternum, stomach, and liver. Examine the various parts of the human brain, and thank God that you have one of each and that the whole thing is connected to the spinal cord. Observe the circulatory system and the cooperation between the skeletal and muscular system. Examine the digestive system, and thank God the next time you have a bowel movement. (Yes, really!) The human body will provide several hours of thanksgiving. Be creative, reflect, and you will "enter his gates with thanksgiving."

But thanksgiving is only one of the dialects of words of affirmation. There is also praise.

Praise, the Cousin of Thanksgiving

The psalmist also challenged us in Psalm 100:4 to enter "his courts with praise." Praise and thanksgiving are cousins. Praise focuses on who God is, while thanksgiving focuses on what God does.

In the Old Testament, the word for *praise* stems from the word *halal,* which is associated with making a noise. Thus Psalm 100 begins with these words, "Make a joyful noise unto the Lord, all ye lands" (KJV). The whole of the Bible is punctuated with outbursts of praise. Praise rises spontaneously from the heart of joy that marks the life of the people of God. The offering of praise (the speaking of praise) is often associated with music. The Hebrew title for the book of Psalms is *Sepher Tehillim,* meaning Book of Praises. The singing of praises was central in both the Old Testament and the New Testament.

Inner joy, which comes from making the God connection, is expressed in praise. Praise, therefore, is a mark of the people of God. Conversely, the heathen are noted by their refusal to praise God.[1]

Verbal and Musical Praise—Some Dialects

Praise to God may be expressed with or without music, in private, or in corporate worship with other praisers. Verbal praise is a way of affirming our belief that God is holy, just, all-powerful, merciful, and loving. He is not only Creator; He is also our Redeemer. He has made possible the love connection and, for that, we praise Him. That we are His children now and forever stimulates praise to God.

If words of affirmation is one's primary love language, it will be easy to express verbal praise to God. But again, one may easily fall into the use of limited phrases and words, expressed at regular times and places. When this happens, even our praise, which started out to be authentic, can become mere ritual. Thus, we enhance our love relationship with God when we think creatively about places and ways to express praise to Him. The Book of Psalms, hymns, and praise choruses all can help stimulate your own creativity as you look for words with which to praise God.

You need not be able to sing well in order to use these tools of praise. Pick up a hymnbook even if you don't consider yourself a musician. Sing one of the old hymns to God. (Don't worry about staying on-key. It does not matter to God.

Remember Psalm 100:1 said, "Make a joyful noise unto the Lord.") After each stanza, express your own words of praise to God. Stand in front of a window looking out on the beauty of God's creation and read aloud Psalm 19. Add your own words of praise after each verse. You may find yourself using words of praise you have never used before. Get a Bible dictionary and look up the word *God*. As you read the article describing the various characteristics of God, express your own words of praise to God for who He is.

Join others in expressing praise to God. This is typically done through music and is called *corporate worship*. Such musical praise brings an added dimension to your affirmations to God. The form of music is relatively unimportant. What is important is that you allow your heart to express itself to God through the words of the songs.

A New Style of Praise

There is much discussion in some Christian circles about the contemporary emphasis on so-called praise and worship music, as opposed to the hymns of the church. Is either better than the other? Perhaps a lesson from history would be helpful for us.

When Isaac Watts was eighteen years old (it was the year 1692), he refused to sing during the church services. One Sunday morning his father rebuked him for not singing. Isaac answered that the music was not worth singing, that the psalms did not rhyme, that they were wooden, awkward in form and phrase. "Those hymns were good enough for your grandfather and father," said the senior Watts, "and they will have to be good enough for you."

"They will never do for me, Father, regardless of what you and your father thought of them."

"If you don't like the hymns we sing, then write better ones," his father said.

"I have written better ones, Father, and if you will relax and listen, I will read one to you." Isaac told his father he had been reflecting on the song of the angels in Revelation 5:6–10 and had rewritten it, giving it rhyme and rhythm. "Behold the glories of the Lamb / Amidst His Father's throne; Prepare new honors for His name / And songs before unknown."

His astonished father took Isaac's composition to the church, and the following Sunday the congregation loved it so much that Isaac was asked to bring another the next Sunday, and the next, and the next, for over two hundred and twenty-two consecutive weeks.[2] Today Isaac Watts is considered the father of modern hymnody.

Expressing the Rhythm and Rhyme of Our Hearts

Three hundred years later, the young Isaac Wattses of our day are writing praise and worship music. The music expresses the rhythm and rhyme of their hearts. Those of us who have been accustomed to the hymns of Isaac Watts would do well to follow the example of Isaac's father and let the youth of our generation lead us into some fresh expressions of praise. In so doing, we may allow them to bless the church for the next three hundred years.

Praise is not a matter of form. It is a matter of the heart. The dialects of praise are many. I suggest that you continue to use those dialects that you have found meaningful in the past and explore the possibility of enhancing your praise of

God by trying new forms. Perhaps a desire to keep one's praise alive and heartfelt also explains why some contemporary young people who have been raised in the more informal, free-flowing styles of worship are finding themselves attracted to the more liturgical worship. The reading of liturgies, which may have become ritual to the one who has repeated them for thirty years, can be like fresh water to the young person who has never heard them. My plea is that we will cease from criticizing styles and forms that are not familiar to us. Instead, let us seek to keep our own praise genuine by searching for ways new to us but known and understood by the God whom we seek to praise.

Other Dialects of Words of Affirmation

I have discussed only two basic dialects of words of affirmation. There are many more. You might try writing God a love letter. (Yes, you can use your computer.) I think God would like this. After all, He wrote you several letters (actually, twenty-one epistles through the apostles). Why not read a chapter in the Bible and listen to what is on His heart, and then write a letter to God expressing your response? If you are poetic, you can write a poem. If you are musical, you can even turn it into a song. If you are a vocalist, you can sing it to God and to others. (If you are not a vocalist, sing it to God alone.)

The dialects for expressing love to God by means of words of affirmation are limitless. You may learn of these dialects by reading the writings of others who have this primary love language. You may learn them from friends in a discussion group, or you may learn them in moments of quiet meditation. With prayer and reflection, asking the great Creator to touch the spirit of creativity within you, you may discover dialects of words of affirmation that have never crossed your mind.

SPEAKING THE LANGUAGE
OF QUALITY TIME

Karen's Quiet Times with God

If your primary love language is quality time, then you will deeply anticipate those moments when you can have time alone with God. You can easily identify with Karen, who said, "The highlight of my day is my 'quiet time' with God." When I inquired about what she did in that "quiet time" with God, she replied, "Usually I read a chapter in the Bible, underline key phrases or words, then talk to God about the words or phrases I have underlined. Sometimes I am asking God questions. Sometimes I am expressing gratitude. Other times I am confessing my sins that were revealed as I read the chapter. Then I typically read a commentary on the chapter to see what others have thought as they read the chapter. Here I sometimes find answers to my questions. Here I am often affirmed to see that others were touched by the same idea that gripped my own mind."

Karen did much more to extend her daily time with God. After the commentary, she read the daily selection in one of her devotional books. Though the subject of the devotional usually was on a totally different topic, Karen reported she found great encouragement in reading the comments of others and their meditations recorded in such books.

"I respond to God about what I read in the devotional," she told me. "Then I have an extended prayer time in which I lay my day, my family, my concerns before Him and ask for

His wisdom and guidance for the day. I sometimes end by singing a song to God. I am not much of a musician, but I think God hears the melody of my heart.

"After my time with God, I am ready to face the day. I talk to Him periodically throughout the day, but that morning 'quiet time' is what sustains my spirit. Without that quality time with Him, my day would be very different. I often compare it to my marriage," Karen said. "When Jim and I have our daily 'couple time' in which we share our lives with each other, I feel connected to him, and our marriage seems healthy. When, for whatever reason, we fail to have these quality times together, I feel distant and often feel there is something wrong in our relationship. The 'quiet time' with God serves the same purpose in my relationship with God. It is what gives me the sense of being close, or intimate, with God."

"Where and when do you spend this quality time with God?" I inquired.

"In the morning before my family wakes up," she said. "It is the only time that really works for me. My place is in the basement at a little table in the corner of the laundry room. Aesthetically, it does not have much to offer, but for me it is a cathedral. Sometimes, as I leave the room I start a load of laundry and look at my sign posted above the washer: 'Remember, you are washing clothes for Jesus.' I discovered that truth in my quiet time with God, from Colossians chapter 3," she said, paraphrasing verse 17.

Perhaps you can identify with Karen. If your primary love language is quality time, you may also have a time, a place, and a method of spending quality time with God, or if you have not yet established a regular "quiet time," you find Karen's description extremely attractive. Karen is speaking the love language of quality time, and for her it is the deepest expression of her love for God and where she most keenly senses His love for her.

"Wonderful Walks Together"

However, there are other dialects of the love language quality time. Patrick is a walker. His personality does not lend itself to the pattern of quality time with God described by Karen. He is a man on the move, but his love language is quality time. When I inquired about how he spent quality time with God, without hesitation he said, "Oh, God and I have wonderful walks together.

"I am committed to memorizing verses of Scripture," he continued. "A friend shared the idea with me, and I have been doing it for several years. I print the verse on the back of one of my business cards. My friend gave me a little leather packet for storing the verse cards. I carry these with me when I walk, and I review the verses, talking to God about each verse.

"Sometimes the verse leads me to confess a sin. Other times I am motivated to cry out for God's help to apply the principle of the verse to my life." And some verses, he explained, stimulate him to pray for other people.

Obviously, Patrick's method of spending quality time with God is quite different from Karen's method, but they are simply different dialects of the same love language. The central element of each is that they are spending quality time in conversation with God.

The City Park and a Home Worship Center

Julia, on the other hand, spoke yet a third dialect of quality time. "My life is so hectic with raising three children and working a full time job and trying to be a wife to Rob. I have never been able to have a daily quiet time with God, though I admit the idea is intriguing to me. So what I have done is carve out one three-hour period each week in which I have extended time with God. Usually it is Thursday morning from 9:00 to 12:00. Thursday is the lightest day in my workweek, and my employer has agreed to give me these three hours off each week—without pay, of course.

"These hours are the highlight of my week. I don't know what I would do if I did not have this extended time to get alone with God. In the summer I go to the city park. There are several picnic tables, and I can always find one that is empty. In the winter I go home. The kids are in school, my husband is at work, and the house is quiet; so I turn our living room into a worship center."

At home Julia sings hymns, reads Scripture, and often reads biographies. Reading about the lives of others encourages her, she reports. "And as I sing and read, I talk to God. I express my worship to Him and I ask for His help and guidance in my life.

"Sometimes I am tempted to do housework during these three hours," Julia confesses. "But thus far, I have not yielded to that temptation. To do so would defeat the whole purpose of spending quality time with God. Someday I hope to be able to have a daily quiet time, but for now this is what works for me. Without it, I am not sure that I would survive the pressures of life. What really encourages me is that I believe God is as excited about our time together as I am. I would feel like I was letting Him down if I did not show up." Obviously, Julia has learned to speak a dialect of quality time that is meaningful to her and enhances her relationship with God.

In One City . . . and Another

Robert was a manufacturer's representative for several companies. He traveled extensively, but I knew him to be a devoted follower of Jesus. I also knew that his primary love language was quality time, so I asked him, "How do you find time to develop your relationship with God when you are on the road all the time?"

"No problem," he said. "Every morning before I leave the hotel room, I spend ten minutes listening and talking to God. I have a little devotional book that I carry in my briefcase. I always read the verse for the day and the comments, and then I talk to God about what I have read and about my day and ask for His guidance.

"Then every evening when the day is over, I am usually in another city, often having dinner with customers. If the weather is nice when dinner is over, I find a public park and take a walk with God, praying about the day, about my family, and about missionaries who are friends of mine. After the walk I sit down and read a chapter in the Bible, underlining those things that seem most important to me and talking with God about them. If the weather does not allow this, then I use the hotel fitness center for some exercise and read the Bible in my room.

"Beginning and ending my day consciously talking to God keeps me close to God. I have been doing this for many years, and I cannot imagine not spending time with God every day. In many ways, it is the most important part of my day. Oh, and after I finish reading the Bible, I call my wife and catch up on what has happened at home. So we have our quality time on the telephone."

OTHER DIALECTS OF QUALITY TIME

I have given four examples of different dialects of the love language quality time, but there are many more. Whatever your lifestyle, if your primary love language is quality time and you genuinely love God, you will find a way to have quality conversations with God. Variety in time, place, and method may well enhance your expressions of love to God by quality time.

For example, if you have a cathedral or church in the city where you live, you might inquire as to the times of day it is open, and, if convenient, you might have your quality time with God in this setting. If you are an indoors person, you might try having quality time with God outdoors, even if the weather is not permitting. Talking to God in the rain can be a new experience. After all, He is the God who sends the rain.

If your schedule is pressured, then skipping lunch and using the time to be alone with God may be the best "steak" you have ever tasted. Making time and finding a place may be difficult in our fast-paced modern world, but the heart that longs for God and the person whose love language is quality time will find a place and the time. Their heart's cry is that of the psalmist, "As the deer pants for streams of water, so my soul pants for you, O God. My soul thirsts for God, for the living God. When can I go and meet with God?"[3]

It is that intense longing of the heart that leads us to be creative in speaking to God the love language of quality time. If quality time is not your primary love language, you may want to learn this language by trying to speak one of the dialects discussed above.

SPEAKING THE LANGUAGE
OF GIFTS

A young couple who had been married only six months once accepted my challenge to give a thousand dollars to our church's annual missions offering by the next Christmas. The plan I suggested was simple. Make the decision, then put aside twenty dollars each week for fifty weeks.

One year later, the couple visited my office with an envelope containing fifty twenty-dollar bills; they planned to put it in the offering plate the next Sunday. They were elated at the joy of giving to God's work around the world.

The wife said, "There were a couple of times that we said to each other, 'Well, if we took some of our mission's money we could do this, but then we both would shake our heads and say, 'No, that is our gift to God. We dare not use it for ourselves.'"

A week or two later, I was visiting in the home of a couple whom I have known for many years; I'll call them Jan and Mike. I had been invited to speak at their church on Sunday morning and was still excited about what was happening in the annual missions offering at my own church, especially this lesson in the joy of giving.

After hearing about the younger couple, Mike said to me, "Let me tell you our story. Before my wife and I were married, each of us had been taught to give 10 percent of our income to God. We had done this as long as we could remember, so when we got married we were in total agreement that we would give 10 percent of all of our income to God."

Grateful Giving

"At the end of the first year, I said to my wife, 'You know, in the Old Testament people gave a tenth of their income, but those of us who have been blessed with the gift of eternal life through Jesus and have the Holy Spirit who gives us power to live our lives should really give more than they gave in the Old Testament.' So I asked Jan what she would think about our increasing our giving to 11 percent, instead of 10. She responded affirmatively, so that year we gave 11 percent. At the end of the year, we had more money left over than we had the year before. So, I suggested to her that since God had blessed us so much, perhaps we should raise our giving to 12 percent.

"She readily agreed, and so it became a pattern of life. Every year we had more left over at the end of the year than we did the year before, so every year we raised our giving by 1 percent."

"How long have you been married?" I inquired.

With a smile he said, "Forty-nine years."

It did not take me long to do the math and realize that he and his wife are now giving 58 percent of their income to God. I could tell it was nothing but sheer joy for the two of them.

More Than Giving Money

However, expressing one's love to God by the love language of gift-giving is not limited to money. Jesus suggested that a cup of cold water given to a thirsty man as an expression of love to God would not go unnoticed by the Father.[4] Loving God is often expressed by meeting the physical needs of His creatures for food, drink, clothing, and shelter. A significant number of those who follow Jesus have always found such giving to be their primary expression of love to God. Nothing delights them more than to be the channel of meeting the physical needs of others. When the local Boy Scout troop makes its annual plea for food for the needy, these people are among the first to respond. When a local radio station is calling for contributions to help those who live in flooded areas, they are the first to respond with clothing and other items.

On the other hand, I have a friend who seldom responds to those kinds of pleas, and yet his primary love language is gift-giving. He is an investor. He regularly takes his biggest gainers and gives them to Christian organizations. Nothing makes him happier. He is able to avoid capital gains taxes by the government by donating stocks, and at the same time he benefits Christian endeavors worldwide. He takes great delight in this double-edged gift-giving.

Giving Encouragement

There is a dialect of gift-giving that has no monetary value at all, but it speaks deeply of one's love for God. It is the gift of encouraging words.

Jim is not a wealthy man. In fact, he lives in a small textile-mill village in a house over seventy years old and in need of repair. His coffers are empty, but his heart is full. He is an exuberant follower of Jesus. In his own words, "I wasted the first fifty years of my life. I allowed alcohol and drugs to control my life. But one night at a rescue mission I turned my life over to Christ, and the leaders of the mission invited me to live on a farm that they operated. The year I spent on the farm totally changed my life. I realized that I did not have to be controlled by alcohol and drugs, but that the Spirit of God wanted to make something good out of my life.

"The last fifteen years of my life have been the best. I have had a steady job. I am buying my own house, and best of all, I have a family of friends at my church who love me. I don't have large sums of money to give to the church, but my friends tell me that does not matter. What I do give is words of encouragement. I take the verses of Scripture that have meant a lot to me over the last fifteen years; I write them on cards and give the cards to people when I feel it is appropriate.

"Many people have told me how much the verses have meant to them. I also pray with people. You know, prayer is a great way to encourage people." Jim is expressing his love to God by giving gifts.

Other Dialects of the Language of Gifts

I have another friend who is a project giver. He gives regularly to his church, but what really excites him is giving to a particular project. Joni Eareckson Tada's Wheels for the World caught his attention. He ended up giving fifteen wheelchairs, but that is just one of the many projects to which he has given through the years. There is something about giving a specific gift for a specific purpose which he can visualize in his mind that makes his giving a greater expression of love to God. He speaks a dialect of gift-giving, with which many people can identify.

Let me suggest that if gift-giving is your primary love language, you consider learning new dialects of giving; expand your horizon by giving in different ways or different things. For those who only give money, consider food. For those who regularly give monetary gifts, consider nonmaterial gifts, such as words of encouragement. With a little creativity, you can expand your primary love language and learn new dialects that will enhance your expressions of love to God. On the other hand, if giving has always been hard for you, pick one of the dialects illustrated above and begin learning the love language of gift-giving.

SPEAKING THE LANGUAGE OF ACTS OF SERVICE

Carl retired twenty years ago from his job as an electrical engineer. Since then, he has built bunk beds at a youth camp in Honduras, a new dining hall and kitchen for a seminary in the Philippines, two new homes for missionaries in Mali, West Africa, remodeled dorms and kitchens at a youth camp in Peru, helped build display cases for a bookstore in Honduras, built a house for a missionary medical doctor in Togo, West Africa, and helped build a base camp for international mission volunteers in Albania.

Why is a "retired" engineer still at work? Because he loves God and his primary love language is acts of service. He uses his abilities to proclaim His love of God and His Son Jesus. In addition to his work in other countries, he has given one year to supervising the building of a sanctuary for a new church in Georgia and another year to doing the same for a church in North Carolina. He has built bookcases for the pastor of a small church in New Jersey, helped remodel classrooms for an academy in Tennessee, and been active in teaching a Bible class in his own church when he wasn't on missions trips.

Carl has only one regret: "I regret I didn't retire sooner, so I could have done more."

Serving by Cooking and Building

Of course, one need not be retired to express love for God by speaking the love language, acts of service. There are many dialects to this language. As long as I have known Marie, her stove has seldom been cold. Her kitchen is her place of worship. She declares her love for God by preparing food for others. When her husband shows up at my door with a meal from Marie, I know that I am the recipient of her love for God. When I am out of town on speaking engagements, if my wife wants food and fellowship, she stops by Marie's for some mint tea and whatever goodies happen to be coming out of her oven that day. Recently Marie provided a meal for her entire Bible fellowship group—forty-six people.

For Marie, such feeding projects are not a burden. They are her delight. It is her way of loving God.

On the other hand, my friend Mark never cooked a meal in his life, but he speaks the acts of service love language fluently. Mark works for the airline industry, but every Christmas and Easter season you will find him on a scaffold high above the choir loft of his church. He is building the set for the Christmas and Easter presentations. For two weeks he takes volunteers and turns them into professional set builders. His finished products would rival Broadway.

Mark's motivation is not money, since he works as a volunteer, nor is it the praise of men. He much prefers to stay in the background. For him, building stage sets is one of the ways he expresses his love to God. Thousands of people are blessed each Christmas and Easter because Mark speaks the love language called acts of service.

Thinking of builders, none is more prolific than Millard Fuller, founder of Habitat for Humanity. I will never forget the first time I met Millard. He is a tall and slender man with the enthusiasm of a winning football coach. By the time he finished his speech, those of us who were volunteers felt that we were about to embark upon the greatest adventure of our lifetime. One week later, when the house was totally finished, we gathered for the dedication and presentation of the house to the new owner.

Millard stood to make the presentation, and with the keys he also presented a Bible in which he had inscribed on the inside cover the following words, which he read for all to hear: "Jesus did many other miraculous signs in the presence of his disciples, which are not recorded in this book. But these are written that you may believe that Jesus is the Christ, the Son of God, and that by believing you may have life in his name."[5]

He said his motivation for founding Habitat for Humanity was to show the love of God and to pray that all men would come to know Jesus Christ in a personal way. I knew that this was not simply a social do-gooder. This was a man deeply in love with God. Habitat for Humanity was his vehicle for speaking the love language acts of service.

Then there is James Lanning. You would not know James, but I will never forget him. Over forty years ago I was pastor of a small church in a small town in North Carolina. James was one of the church deacons. He was an electrician by trade, but he was also a plumber. He pulled me aside one day and said, "Now, preacher, when your house or the church needs any plumbing or electrical work, don't you call a plumber or electrician; you call me. I can't do much for the Lord, but I can do plumbing and electrical work. That's my way of saying thank you to God for all He has done for me. You hear?"

I heard, and when I had electrical or plumbing needs I called James. It was a joy to watch him love God.

People whose primary love language is acts of service take whatever skills they have and use them to do the work of God. They are following their leader of whom it was said, "He went around doing good."[6] They are not all technically skilled people, but they are worker bees, raking leaves, cleaning gutters, removing snow, delivering meals. They are reaching out to serve others as an expression of their love for God.

Recently while in the grocery store, I encountered a mother and her three children, ages eight, ten, and twelve. When I asked, "What are you and the children doing this summer?" she replied, "One day a week we all go downtown to the local soup kitchen and help serve lunch and clean up afterwards. The children love it and it's something I've always wanted to do."

Because I had counseled with her and her husband several years earlier, I knew that her primary love language was acts of service. It was encouraging to see her expressing her love to God in this manner.

It was also encouraging to see that she was teaching her children to speak this love language. I must admit that most of the mothers I meet in the summer are taking their children to the swimming pool or to a sports event. How refreshing to see a mother teaching her children to love God by loving others. Keep in mind there are many worthwhile programs like this, including Meals on Wheels, which involves taking meals to the elderly and sick.

If acts of service is your primary love language, let me encourage you to learn new dialects and enhance your love relationship with God. Try being a teacher's aide, going on a mission trip, or volunteering at your local church or hospital. Your opportunities are limited only by your willingness to explore. If acts of service is not your native language, then begin with a simple project and develop your vocabulary in learning to love God by serving others.

SPEAKING THE LANGUAGE OF PHYSICAL TOUCH

Touching the "Untouchables"

At age seventeen, Lisa went to Los Angeles on a short-term missions trip. While there she became burdened for prostitutes, women whom most of society would rather not think about. Sensing God's call on her life, she enrolled at Moody Bible Institute in Chicago. She chose as her major urban ministries and began to search for an organization that ministered to prostitutes, but no such ministry existed.[7]

So Lisa started one: Salvage House. Every night from 9 P.M. until 1 A.M., Lisa and a teammate walked the streets of Chicago looking for prostitutes to whom they could minister. Two male team members followed them for protection. Lisa's approach was simple: Build relationships and provide a safe place where the women's physical and spiritual needs could be met. In Lisa's Salvage House, women for whom physical touch had been a means of exploitation discovered the warm embrace of truly loving arms. During the past few years, the caring touch of Lisa and her teammates has helped many women experience the love of God.

Every society has its category of *untouchable* people. In first-century Palestine, they were the lepers and prostitutes. The lepers lived apart from the rest of society and were compelled to cry aloud "unclean, unclean" when they realized that another person was approaching them. The prostitutes were so abhorred that the religious leaders concluded that Jesus could not be a prophet and allow such a woman to "wet his feet with her tears ... [wipe] them with her hair, [kiss] them and [pour] perfume on them."[8]

In Western society we also have our untouchables. We would not be so brazen as to publish the categories, but by our behavior we demonstrate that certain people are not to be touched. The categories differ from individual to individual. For some it's prostitutes; for others it's people with the deadly disease of AIDS. Some dread those commonly called "street people"; others avoid "sex offenders," the mentally incompetent, physically grotesque, or spiritually cultish.

The love of God cuts across all of these man-made barriers. And those who are truly in love with Him will be His agents for touching the untouchables.

Some weeks ago, I was talking to a long-term friend whom I had not seen for some time. Earlier while attending one of my seminars with his wife, he told me his primary love language was physical touch. When I asked the question, "What are you doing exciting this summer?" his response was immediate.

"My son, Bobby, and I have been going to the rescue mission every Monday night. It has been so exciting. We shake hands with all the men as they come into the mission; we pat them on the back and hug them; for those who come for prayer at the end of the service, we bow on our knees beside them, put our arms on their shoulders, and pray for them.

"Some of my friends say they can't believe that we are doing this, but for Bobby and me it's the most exciting part of our summer. I know that most of these men do not get many handshakes, hugs, and pats on the back. I feel like we are being God's representatives to show God's love to them."

I did not ask if physical touch was also his son Bobby's primary love language, but one thing is certain: Bobby is learning to speak that language fluently as he and his father touch the untouchables.

Fearful of Touching Others?

It is often the fear of disease that keeps people from touching the untouchables. "I don't want to get close to AIDS patients. I'm afraid I'll get it," is an all-too-common attitude. I'm not suggesting that in our efforts to love we minimize the dangers (though you will not get AIDS by giving a hug or clasping a shoulder). I did ask Bobby's father about his concerns for their physical health. "Well," he said, "we try to take normal precautions. We wash our hands before we go to the rescue mission. We are careful not to put our hands near our noses or mouths. We wash our clothes and take a shower as soon as we get home. So far we haven't had any problems."

Learning and following good health habits is extremely important, particularly for those who work with people who have communicable diseases, but we must not allow ungrounded fear to keep us from expressing love to God by touching His creatures who live on the edges of society.

Touching in Institutional Settings

A few days later I encountered Mary, a mother who was taking her thirteen-year-old daughter once a week to an assisted living complex for aging adults. "What do you do?" I inquired.

"Mostly we just love them," she said.

"And how do you express this love?" I asked.

"I think one of the most important things we do is touch

these people," she said. "It's amazing how many of them extend their hand when we walk by. They're eager for a handshake. When we get ready to leave the room after our visit, those who are able often stand up and reach out for a hug. Of course, whether they reach out or not, I hug them. You know me; I'm a hugger." For Mary, hugging is a way of expressing love.

People who live in institutional settings, such as nursing homes, prisons, and extended-stay hospitals, often are deprived of loving physical touches. Some do not have relatives who visit, and those who do may have relatives who are not "touchers." Thus, they are extremely open to anyone who will express love to them by physical touch. Mary reported, "I have never had anyone turn away from me or draw back from my hugging them. I get the feeling that they look forward to our coming because they know they are going to get a hug."

Prayer and Physical Touch

Of course, expressing love to God by physically touching His children is not limited to those living in institutional settings. Jim is a pray-er. For him, praying for people is the most powerful thing one can do. If you share a prayer request with him, he will not write it on a sheet of paper to be prayed for later. He will say, "Let's pray about that now."

When Jim prays for people, he always makes physical contact with the person. For some he extends his hand. For others he puts his hand on their shoulder as he prays.

His prayers are simple but intense. When he finishes praying, he typically pats the person on the back and embraces him.

One man said to me, "When Jim puts his arm on my shoulder and prays for me, I feel like God has put His arm on my shoulder and is listening intently to what Jim is saying." Obviously for this man, Jim's physical touch is the touch of God.

Hugging

King Brown is eighty-two years old, and a few months ago he invited Karolyn and me to join him and his wife for dinner. A week after his telephone call we were in a restaurant with King and Frances, his bride of more than fifty years.

King wore a suit and tie, and on his suit coat was the badge he has been wearing every time I've seen him for thirty years. It said, "Hugging is a contact sport."

King and Frances told us the story of their courtship and wedding. We talked about their five boys and their families. In the midst of our conversation, a lady with whom Karolyn and I have been acquainted many years stepped to the table to say hello. I proceeded to introduce her to King and Frances, at which time he stood up and reached out to hug the lady. Her response was immediate and straightforward. She stepped back and said, "The only man I allow to hug me is my husband."

King, obviously shocked, sat back down and said, "I can appreciate that." The lady proceeded to explain her rationale, and he again affirmed that he could appreciate that.

When she left, King said to us, "In over sixty years of hugging, she's the second person who has ever refused a hug. I guess two in sixty years is not so bad."

We have known King and Frances for over thirty years. I have never known anyone who speaks the love language of physical touch more fluently than he. As we left the restaurant,

I was encouraged to see the way he helped Frances get her coat on, patted her on the back, and held her hand as they walked to the car. After five children and fifty years of marriage, he still expresses his love by affectionate touch.

His chief dialect of physical touch is hugging people. Young or old, male or female, married or single, if they encounter him they will be hugged. And if they engage him in conversation, in less than five minutes he will be talking about God. As long as I have known him, King has been passionately in love with God.

King once told me, "You'd be surprised how many people tell me that my hug is the first hug they've had in a month. I don't think people realize how powerful it is to give a hug." I think King is right, and I also agree that two refusals in sixty years of hugging is not a bad record.

When you understand that people are made in the image of God and that God loves them intensely and that you are His representative on the earth to express that love, physical touch becomes more than a social grace. It becomes a most meaningful expression of God's love. If physical touch is your primary love language, I hope that you can be "God's arm" on the shoulder of many people.

Proper Touching

In a culture where sexual exploitation has become so commonplace, I am compelled to say that true expressions of love via physical touch should always be for the benefit of the person touched. If the motive is to manipulate, and thus satisfy your own sensual desires, physical touch ceases to be an expression of love. Those who use the love language of physical touch for the purpose of exploitation have ceased to be vehicles of God's love.

Let me also add that although such exploitation is becoming common in contemporary culture, we must not allow our fear of being misinterpreted to keep us from speaking the authentic love language of physical touch.

A friend of mine recently returned from Kenya in eastern Africa. He told me of his conversation with a lady whose husband had become a Christian. He asked, "What is the greatest change you noticed when your husband became a follower of Jesus?" to which the lady responded without hesitation, "He stopped beating me." Those who are true followers of Jesus will never use physical touch as a means of harming others but will view it as a vehicle of expressing God's love to others.

The purpose of this chapter is to encourage you to enhance your love relationship with God by using new dialects of your primary love language and perhaps exploring the possibility of learning to speak a second or third love language to God. It is my hope that in speaking new languages and dialects, your love relationship with God will continue to grow and be forever vibrant.

9

WHEN LOVE
SEEMS DISTANT

$\mathcal{R}$EAL LOVE INCLUDES DISCIPLINE. If we love, we will correct. When psychiatrist Ross Campbell and I wrote our book *The Five Love Languages of Children,* we included a chapter on love and discipline, noting that truly loving parents will of necessity bring discipline to the child's life. Helping children learn to live within parameters is an essential part of preparing them to live as responsible citizens in an adult world.

We made two key observations. First, a child is most likely to rebel against discipline when the child's emotional love tank is empty. Thus, we encouraged parents to speak the child's primary love language before and after the disciplinary action. Second, we observed that the child is most sensitive to the method of discipline that is related to his primary love language. If, for example, the child's primary love language is words of affirmation, then words which condemn the child's behavior will be felt deeply by the child. When a child is experiencing such discipline, he may feel estranged from the parents and even conclude that the parents do not love him.[1]

GOD'S LOVING DISCIPLINE

The child's struggle in understanding parental discipline often becomes the adult's struggle in understanding the discipline of God. The same two principles seem to be true. First, *we are most likely to rebel against the discipline of God when our spiritual love tank is empty.* If we do not feel God's love, then His discipline may seem to be extremely harsh. Second, *when God's method of discipline relates directly to our primary love language, it strikes us at the deepest possible level.*

Discipline to Bring Us Back to God

When do we most need God's discipline? Answer: When we are walking away from God and are in danger of bringing harm to ourselves and others. This also parallels the parent/child relationship. However, when we are walking away from God, we are less likely to feel His love. A sense of "distance" develops between us and our Creator. Consequently, when He reaches out to discipline us, we often interpret His methods as being severe.

We may accuse God of being unfair, but in reality it was our movement away from Him that brought "the distance." When we walk in intimate fellowship with God, His discipline is much more likely to be interpreted as an act of love rather than judgment.

Since we are by nature most sensitive to the discipline that relates directly to our primary love language, God often uses that love language to bring us to a place of repentance and forgiveness. When we are on a destructive pathway and God really wants to get our attention, He often disciplines us in keeping with our primary love language.

For example, if our primary love language is words of affirmation, then the heavens become silent. On earth, our work colleagues begin to deliver messages of condemnation. At home, the spouse and children become critical. When we open the Bible, our eyes are drawn to those statements that reveal our sinfulness. We read the words of the prophet Nathan indicting King David, "You are the man!" and we know they are the words of God to us. Our hearts are empty, and in desperation we cry out to God and begin our journey homeward.

Discipline for Our Good

God knows us better than we know ourselves. He knows how to get our attention. His discipline is not always pleasant, but it is always purposeful. The author of the New Testament book of Hebrews knew this reality when he penned these words:

> "My son, do not make light of the Lord's discipline, and do not lose heart when he rebukes you, because the Lord disciplines those he loves, and he punishes everyone he accepts as a son."
>
> Endure hardship as discipline; God is treating you as sons. For what son is not disciplined by his father? . . . Our fathers disciplined us for a little while as they thought best; but God disciplines us for our good, that we may share in his

holiness. No discipline seems pleasant at the time, but painful. Later on, however, it produces a harvest of righteousness and peace for those who have been trained by it.[2]

The overarching principle is clear. God always disciplines us for our good. On the human level, parents disciplined us in keeping with what they believed to be for our good. But parents are not perfect and sometimes make mistakes. God, on the other hand, is holy, and His discipline toward us is always for our ultimate good. His discipline is seldom pleasant and sometimes extremely painful, but His purpose is to move us down the pathway of righteousness and peace.

These two words, *righteousness* and *peace,* must never be separated. Peace, which means literally "to be at one with," is at the heart of man's desire. Most of us deeply desire "inner peace." We want our emotions, thoughts, desires, and actions to relate to each other harmoniously. The opposite of inner peace is anxiety. We also desire peace in human relationships. So many people have said to me through the years, "I would give everything I own simply to have harmony with my spouse," or in some cases, "with my children." The desire of all thinking people is that societies may live together in harmony. Many of the world's religions have as the central motif the idea of peace—being in harmony with the universe. However, for most, religious or nonreligious, this dream is elusive.

SEEING DISCIPLINE AS
AN ACT OF GOD'S LOVE

The reality is there can be no peace on any level of human existence if we are not living in keeping with the Creator's design. In the Scriptures this is called living righteously. It is choosing the right path, choosing to obey the rules of God because we believe that they are designed for our well-being. When we walk in righteousness, we experience peace. This is always God's desire for us, and His discipline is designed to move us to this ideal. Knowing this does not remove the pain of discipline, but it does help us interpret the discipline as an act of God's love.

Numb with Sorrow

R. G. LeTourneau (whom we met in chapter 4) illustrates the two principles discussed above: (1) God's discipline seems harsh when we don't feel His love, and (2) It will affect us most directly when He uses our love language in discipline. As a young Christian man trying to get his business off the ground, LeTourneau became consumed with business and began moving away from God. When his eldest son died, he interpreted it as the severe discipline of God.

In his autobiography, LeTourneau described his response:

> I held Evelyn, but when I could find words, it was to God that I addressed them. "What is wrong?" I pleaded. "What have we done that we should be so punished? We have worked hard. We have tried our best to be Christians. Oh, where have we gone wrong?"
>
> That night, while we were still numb with sorrow, the answer came to me. "My child," the Voice said, "you have been working hard, but for the wrong things. You have been working for material things. . . ."
>
> The words were few, but the meaning ran deep. All that long night I reviewed my past and saw where I had been

paying only token tribute to God, going through the motions of acting like a Christian, but really serving myself and my conscience, instead of serving Him. Instead of being a humble servant, I was taking pride in the way I was working to pay my material debts at the garage, while doing scarcely a thing to pay my spiritual debt to God.

From my lesson that night, I can now say that when a man realizes that spiritual things are worth more—and certainly they will last when material things are gone—he will work harder for spiritual things. I discovered then that God loves us so much that He wants us to love Him in return. He wants us to cooperate with His program. . . . That I had not been doing. I had been seeking first my own way of life, and I firmly believe that God had to send those difficulties into our lives to get us to look up into His face and call upon Him for His help and guidance.[3]

When God Disciplines in Our Love Language

LeTourneau's primary love language was gifts. He considered his children God's choicest gifts; thus, when that gift was taken away, God got his undivided attention. Nothing could have spoken more deeply to the soul of R. G. LeTourneau. God's discipline was directly related to his primary love language. LeTourneau responded positively to the discipline of God, and from that moment his life took a different course. He walked "in righteousness and peace." He went on to accomplish the unusual successes that we recounted in chapter 4, but God was forever the focus of his life and work. One must wonder if LeTourneau's life would have accomplished so much for God and good in the world without the severe discipline of God early in his life.

For those whose primary love language is gifts, answered prayer is strong, emotional evidence of God's love. Thus, in the early years of their spiritual journey, they may become troubled and even angry at God when they do not receive the good gifts for which they pray. When their prayers seem to go unanswered, their faith in God is shaken. When tragedy enters their lives, they tend to think that God has been unfair. They struggle more deeply with unanswered prayer and tragedy than do other believers. But in their maturing years, they come to see even these things as true gifts from God. They come to understand that loving parents do not always grant the requests of their children. The reason? Because they love them too much to grant those things they know will be harmful to their children.

So God's refusal to give His children all that they request is not a withdrawal of His love but rather a profound expression of His love. What appears to be tragedy is often God's loudest expression of love.

Megan's primary love language is quality time. I first met her when she was a student at the university, majoring in religious studies. She had a deep passion for God and would spend hours in contemplation, meditation, and prayer. Conversations with her were always stimulating, and fellow students looked up to her as somewhat of a spiritual guide. After graduation from the university, she spent two years working with a mission organization in South America. Later she returned and completed a master's degree in counseling.

About halfway through this program, she started dating a young man who not only had no time for religion; he actually prided himself in being agnostic. He was convinced that no one could be certain of God's existence, and he spent a great deal of his time trying to convince others of his uncertainty.

As Megan told me the story six years later, "I fell in love with him, and before I knew it, I too was doubting the existence of God. I stopped having my daily devotional times with God, and I started attending meetings with my boyfriend where people discussed an intellectual approach to life without a belief in God. At first I thought I could be a positive influence on him and his friends, but as time went on I realized that they were having an influence on me. I noticed I was spending more time reading books recommended by him than I was reading Scripture.

"I had this growing sense of emptiness and one day realized that I was living only to be with my boyfriend and that our being together was the focus of my life. When he finally left me for another girl, I was devastated. By this time I had completed my master's degree at the university in counseling, and I realized that I was in a deep, clinical depression. Even when I tried to pray, it seemed like God wasn't listening. I felt so far from God that I wondered if I had committed 'the unpardonable sin.'

"I got treatment for my depression and in about six months I came out of it. But I still felt so far away from God. In my heart I knew He was there, but the depression had left me with so many memories of loneliness that I wondered if I could ever experience God's presence again. It was about this time that a friend invited me to a Bible study at her house. I went because I wanted to be around Christians again. They were beginning a series of studies for new Christians so I signed up for the weekly classes."

Megan called the next three months "the most important of my life." She had been deprived of experiencing God in her primary love language, quality time. Now, like the "deer [that] pants for streams of water," Megan yearned for God, "to go and meet with God."[4] She brought the class workbook home and said to God, "I want to start over as though I were just beginning my relationship with You. Teach me of Your love."

"It was like coming home from a long journey," Megan told me. "Day by day as I did my study in the Scriptures, I rediscovered the love of God. I realized the futility of life apart from Him. The highlight of my day was the time spent reading the Scriptures and talking to God. That was two years ago, and I continue to meet with my study group every week. We have gone through numerous studies together. I now have a job as a full-time counselor, and I've never been happier in my life."

My conversation with Megan happened over fifteen years ago. Today she is one of the finest counselors I know. One of her specialties is helping people understand and process depression. Approximately five years after our conversation, Megan married and since then has given birth to two children. Since the children came, her counseling has been limited to two days a week, but her passion for God has never wavered. In her own words, "The severe discipline of depression was the most significant event in my life. I shudder to think what would have happened to me if I had continued on the road I was walking. It was the desperation of depression that brought me back to God. As painful as it was, I sincerely thank God for the experience."

God loves us enough to stay away from us if that is what it takes to create a fresh hunger for His presence. For those whose primary love language is quality time, this is often His method of discipline.

"ISN'T GOD GOOD?"

Sometimes God's discipline seems harshest when our hopes or expectations go unfulfilled. At those times we must remember God is good. He still loves us. I remember Cindy, whom I met at a large single adult conference in the mountains of North Carolina. She said, "I used to think that God didn't love me because He hadn't given me a husband. I prayed diligently for 'the right man,' but the years came and went and God never answered my prayer. I often felt that God did not love me as much as He did my friends. But then, one by one, I saw my friends after seven, ten, twelve years of marriage divorce. I saw the pain that they endured. I saw the trauma created in the lives of their children. The pain they endured was far deeper than the pain I had endured in my singleness.

"I remember the day I said to God, 'It's OK, Father. In fact, thank You for not answering my prayer in giving me a husband. I realize now that I would have been too immature to have made a success of a marriage. Thank You for the gift of singleness.' I can honestly say that I am happy to be single. I don't feel that God has slighted me but has loved me intently and preserved me from tragedy."

Within a year of that conversation, I got a letter from Cindy. "Dear Dr. Chapman, I am writing to say that God has finally brought into my life the right man. I really wasn't anticipating marriage. I'm sure you remember our conversation, but it just happened. I met Kevin shortly after I left the conference last year. He had only arrived in our city about a month earlier and immediately joined our singles' group at church. We became friends three months before we dated. And our relationship has been everything I ever dreamed. Kevin is truly a Christian gentleman. Isn't God good?"

Cindy and Kevin have been married for ten years now; they have two children and a delightful relationship. They periodically lead marriage enrichment groups in their church. Cindy once said to me, "God gives good gifts to His children but only when He knows they are ready to receive them."

DOES A LOVING GOD HEAL US?

When Pain Persists

Physical pain and debilitating disease have often stimulated this question in the minds of those who seek to follow God: *If God is love, then why does He allow His children to suffer such intense pain?* In grappling with this difficult question, sincere Christians have come to different conclusions. Some propose that all sickness and suffering is from Satan, that it is never God's will for His people to experience disease. If Satan brings sickness, then the prayer of faith will bring healing. While there are legitimate testimonies of divine healing, there are at the same time thousands whose faith has been shattered because they "prayed in faith" and were not healed.

It is true that the Scriptures instruct believers to pray for the healing of the sick, but it is not true that God has categorically committed Himself to heal every person whose level of faith is sufficient. In the Scriptures, healing is never based on man's power to believe but rests solidly in the hands of the sovereign God who chooses to heal or not to heal, always choosing for our good and the good of others.

Paul's Chronic Affliction

Paul, the first-century apostle whose conversion to Christ we explored in chapter 6, became the greatest leader of the early Christian church. It could be argued that he was the most godly of the godly, but his life was not spared the suffering of pain. He was often thrown in prison and flogged severely. Three times he was stoned and left for dead, once shipwrecked and left to the sharks, often robbed of his meager belongings. None of this seemed to trouble Paul deeply, but he did struggle when his body was afflicted with disease. Three times Paul pleaded with God for healing, but God's answer was, "My grace is sufficient for you, for my power is made perfect in weakness." Upon reflection, Paul concluded that his illness was to keep him from being conceited because of the great revelations God had given him. He clearly saw his sickness as God's positive, loving discipline. "Therefore," he said, "I will boast all the more gladly about my weaknesses, so that Christ's power may rest on me. That is why, for Christ's sake, I delight in weaknesses, in insults, in hardships, in persecutions, in difficulties. For when I am weak, then I am strong."[5]

Paul's primary love language was probably physical touch. His conversion had been precipitated by the presence of God touching his body, leaving him blind for three days. After his conversion, he was a man on the move, certainly the greatest missionary of the Christian church. Physically he poured out his life as an expression of love for Christ, the One who had touched him and turned his life around. In the midst of fruitful ministry, God used the loving discipline of physical touch to keep Paul on track so that the latter portion of his life would be fully as effective as the early years following his conversion.

At the end of his life Paul could say, "The time has come

for my departure. I have fought the good fight, I have finished the race, I have kept the faith."[6] God's discipline had served its purpose, and Paul had nothing but gratitude to the God who cared enough to bring loving discipline.

DEALING WITH A CRISIS OF FAITH

When Physical Touch Is the Primary Love Language

Throughout history many of God's choice leaders have experienced the pain of disease. Typically, such an experience draws our attention to God, particularly after the medical professionals have done all they can do and the disease persists. Sickness is often God's E-mail to turn our attention in a different direction. But for those whose primary love language is physical touch, it is God's megaphone. They're touched more deeply and their lives more profoundly changed than others who have a different love language.

I met Clarence over forty years ago. He appeared at church in a wheelchair, afflicted with multiple sclerosis. As the years came and went, his disease progressed in spite of numerous prayers for healing. Eventually he became bedridden, and in the last fifteen years of his life he could no longer move his arms and legs. The only movement which he could control was his neck.

The local library arranged an apparatus that could hold a book above the bed and the pages could be turned as he put his chin on a metal bar, thus allowing him to read. A friend also arranged a similar mechanism whereby Clarence could turn on the radio by the same chin movement. Thus he had contact with the outside world by a radio and books.

Periodically I visited Clarence, and we had numerous extended conversations. Some of those focused on God's purposes in allowing him to suffer from multiple sclerosis.

In the early years Clarence struggled greatly with why God had allowed this to happen to him. He had completed college and seminary in preparation for ministry and soon had a pastorate, but his preaching ministry was cut short, and he had difficulty understanding that. As Paul the apostle prayed for healing, so Clarence prayed for healing. But again, as with Paul, the healing he desired did not come. What did come was a growing awareness that God had a different kind of ministry for him, one that focused not on preaching but on praying.

Clarence became one of the greatest men of prayer I have ever known. As he listened to the radio, he prayed for the individual behind the voice and for the people who heard the message. Every page of every book brought to mind people for whom he needed to pray. Once the word got out that Clarence was a prayer warrior, requests came from many quarters. I often shared my own needs and always knew in my heart that, for him, prayer requests were never a burden, but a ministry.

For twenty-five years, Clarence had an unparalleled ministry of prayer, the results of which only eternity will reveal. First seated in his chair and later prone on his bed, he had his understanding opened. God used the megaphone of physical touch to channel Clarence's life into the most productive ministry possible for him.

When Acts of Service Is the Primary Love Language

There are other individuals for whom acts of service is their primary love language. When these people make the God connection and experience God's love and forgiveness, they will most often express their love to God by serving others in Jesus' name. When that service is thwarted or taken away from them, they will experience a crisis of faith. As one young lady said, "What is God doing? I'm trying to serve Him. Why would He allow this to happen?" Obviously, God had her full attention, but she was not sure what God was saying.

Robert grew up in a home where his father was an electronics recluse. He worked for a manufacturer of electronic equipment, taught electronics at the local community college, and spent all of his spare time in his electronic shop in the basement of his house. Robert seldom had the attention of his father. His mother complained about his father's lifestyle and spent much of her time depressed. She was extremely domineering and controlling of Robert's life. In his teenage years, Robert began to realize that he was sexually attracted to young men, and by the time he was eighteen he was actually involved in a homosexual relationship.

College for Robert was his dream of deliverance. He could hardly wait to get away from the pain of his disinterested father and dominating mother. He saw the college campus as an opportunity to explore his sexuality and enjoy his independence. However, six weeks into the first semester Robert found himself very lonely and depressed. Little did Robert know that his life was about to take a radical turn.

Julia was a bubbly freshman turned on to Jesus and into helping people. She invited Robert to join her in her Meals on Wheels project every Wednesday at noon. Robert didn't have classes on Wednesdays, so he was eager to help. Later she got him involved in building a Habitat for Humanity house, and in the fall she pulled him into a leaf-raking, gutter-cleaning project sponsored by her Bible study group. Before the first semester was over, Robert was attending the Bible study group, and in the second semester he made the God connection.

As he put it, "Julia worked me into the arms of Jesus. I loved helping people and I also loved the way Julia helped me with my math class. I really needed help. She seemed to genuinely care about me. Later, when she told me that she loved me because God first loved her, and that she enjoyed helping me because God had helped her, I was interested in this God.

"When I finally discovered what God had already done for me when He sent Christ to take my death rap, I knew that He loved me, and I knew that I must respond to His love."

Clearly, Robert's love language was acts of service, but in loving God, Robert didn't know what to do about his homosexual lifestyle. As he continued to study the Bible, he realized that homosexuality was not God's plan of sexual expression, but why did he have these strong attractions for other men? With ambivalent feelings, he eventually shared his struggles with Julia. He feared that she might reject him if she knew.

Her initial response shocked him. She gave him the longest, hardest hug he had ever received from anyone, and she said, "Oh, Robert. I'm so glad you are being honest with me. There is hope. God can take care of your problem." Robert wasn't sure of that, but he was willing to give God a chance. Julia introduced Robert to her pastor, who in turn referred him to a Christian counselor who not only helped Robert understand his sexual feelings but affirmed Julia's belief that distorted sexual feelings, like other distorted emotions, could be changed.

For Robert, it was a life-changing journey. His journey led not only to the diminishing of his attraction to the same sex, but to the discovery and development of heterosexual feelings. Robert continued with Julia to be active in the Bible study group and their acts of service to the community.

Upon graduation, he and Julia married and headed off to seminary. Robert believed that God wanted him to be a minister.

While in seminary, Robert had a part-time job as a social worker while Julia worked for a local bank. They were both actively involved in the Hispanic ministry of their church. Upon graduation, Robert was eager to begin his full-time ministry, using his primary love language in service for Christ. When he was called to a small-town church in Virginia, he was overjoyed with the prospects of the future. However, his joy was turned to tears three years later when the church asked him to resign. In his efforts to help others, Robert had been honest about his earlier struggles with homosexuality. When the deacons learned of this, they did not want such a man to be their pastor. Robert suffered the pain of rejection for being honest.

Robert's faith was greatly shaken—not only his faith in the Christians to whom he ministered but in God Himself. "How could God let this happen when I tried so hard to walk in honesty and integrity before Him?" He wondered whether God had forsaken him. He had come to the church that he might serve God; now his opportunity for service was gone. Where was God in all of this?

What Robert did not know and could not have known then was that God had far different plans for his life. Today, Robert leads a thriving ministry to men and women who have suffered from same-sex attraction disorder. Many of them lived an active homosexual or lesbian lifestyle but have made the God connection and are coming to grips with the power of God to change lives. It is not a ministry which he would have chosen for himself. His desire would have been to see that portion of his life as history and to use his energy to pastor a "normal" church.

What Robert is discovering is that he was being uniquely prepared of God for the ministry in which he is now involved. But it took the discipline of taking away his "normal" ministry in order to channel him into God's designed ministry for him.

Was the experience painful? Yes. Were the deacons violating Christian principles in their action? Yes. But God used all of it to speak deeply to Robert's spirit and open his heart to the ministry for which God had prepared him.

Sometimes our sincere efforts at loving God by serving others will be thwarted—perhaps by the direct act of Satan, perhaps by well-meaning Christians. But behind all of that is the hand and voice of God, moving His children in the best direction for them. For those whose primary love language is acts of service, this can be God's most severe loving discipline. However, it may be the only discipline which would deeply get our attention and motivate us to seek God's new directions for our expressions of love to Him.

When Words of Affirmation Is the Primary Love Language

Brad spoke a different love language. He thrived on words of affirmation. During junior high school, he took a few guitar lessons, and as a high school freshman he was invited to join a rock band. Brad felt accepted and approved by the band members. Though they only played at a few birthday parties, his parents always gave him words of affirmation about his musical abilities. The band tried to put together a demo tape but were never able to succeed. And by the beginning of his junior year, the group disbanded.

Brad went on to other pursuits, but in college he returned to his musical interest and decided to major in music education. Although his parents encouraged him verbally, he did not receive much encouragement from his teachers. And his musical career floundered. Eventually Brad decided to major in business, and his grades greatly improved.

Brad never gave much thought to God or spiritual matters, but after graduation, he secured a job with a small company owned and operated by passionate Christians. They opened the offices each morning with prayer. The place was permeated with the spirit of excitement and encouragement. Brad heard more about God in the first six months of employment than he had heard his whole life. There was something about all of this that intrigued him. These people seemed to be extremely happy, and they were very complimentary of his work.

It was in this context that Brad began to read the Bible for himself. He began by reading the life of Jesus as recorded by John the apostle. He was enamored by the words of Jesus, especially His description as "the good shepherd [who] lays down his life for the sheep." Brad read that Jesus claimed "the reason my Father loves me is that I lay down my life—only to take it up again. No one takes it from me, but I lay it down of my own accord. I have authority to lay it down and authority to take it up again."[7] *Could Jesus really be foretelling His own death and resurrection?* Brad wondered.

Later he read Jesus' words to Martha, the sister of Lazarus. "I am the resurrection and the life," Jesus said. "He who believes in me will live, even though he dies."[8] By the time Brad neared the end of the Gospel According to John, he was ready for these words: "Jesus did many other miraculous signs in the presence of his disciples, which are not recorded in this book.

But these are written that you may believe that Jesus is the Christ, the Son of God, and that by believing you may have life in his name."

In Brad's words, "Something deep within me responded and I said aloud, 'I believe.' In that moment, my life was changed forever." Brad had made the God connection.

The next six months were a tremendous adventure as Brad exposed himself to the teachings of Scripture. He decided to attend his employer's church, where he immediately enrolled in a class for new Christians. Soon he began to learn to share his life with God.

"I'll never forget the time I first prayed," Brad said. "I began, 'Dear God, I don't know much about talking to You, but if You're willing to listen, I do have some questions I'd like to ask.' I've been asking questions, and He's been answering ever since," Brad said.

The part of the worship service Brad enjoyed most was the music. He was singing words he had never sung before, and they were expressing the true feelings of his heart. Before long, he got the idea that perhaps he should join the choir. Words of affirmation was his primary love language, but at the first rehearsal, he discovered he didn't have the gift of singing.

"I'll never forget the first night Brad came to rehearsal," the music minister would say later. "I knew he was there because I heard him before I saw him. He was off-key and out of rhythm."

When the music director realized that Brad really wanted to sing in the choir, he took some private time to try to help him, but he soon realized that Brad wasn't going to make it. He was kind but honest as he suggested Brad needed to find another area of ministry.

Brad's response? "That was the most devastating experience I had encountered since becoming a Christian. At first,
I thought the music minister was out of line. Hadn't I been
a part of a rock band in high school? Didn't I major in music when I first started college? What did he mean when he
said I didn't have 'the gift of singing'? Later a couple of friends
confirmed the music minister's diagnosis, and I came to accept my musical limitations.

"I think the reason I found it so difficult was that I saw
singing as a way of expressing praise to God. I realize now
what I didn't realize then. I was right, but if I wanted to sing
words of praise to God, I should do it in private rather than
distracting fellow worshipers by singing off-key."

All of this happened many years ago. Brad went on to
become a successful businessman. As for his love language,
words of affirmation, he became one of the best Bible teachers ever to be a member of his church. For the past twenty
years, his classes have always been well attended. People bring
friends and they are never disappointed. Brad's classes are
creative, alive, and insightful.

Words of affirmation is still his love language, and he expresses his love to God by teaching the truth of God to hundreds of people every year. It was the loving discipline of
painful words from a music minister (and ultimately God) that
got Brad's attention and steered him in the right direction.

Those of us who, like Brad, have the primary love language
of words of affirmation will find critical or corrective words
very painful. But if we seek to hear the voice of God, we may
discover that such words are His loudest expressions of love
to us. Once God has us where we need to be, we will again
hear the affirming words of those to whom we minister.

God's discipline is not always in response to our sinful

behavior. Often it is His effort to direct our sincere efforts to worship and serve Him in a more productive manner. Though our initial response may be to recoil in pain and question what God is doing, if we ask our honest questions and listen for "the still small voice" of God, we will likely find that in our moments of deepest pain God is loving us most intensely.

10

WHEN LOVE PREVAILS

I FIRST MET MICHAEL CASSIDY while seated in the breathtakingly beautiful Sheldonian Theater at Oxford University in England. He was introduced as one of the top twenty people in South Africa who eased the transition from apartheid to free elections. I was captivated by his story.

"I came to Cambridge to study law, but within two weeks I encountered Christ. Billy Graham came to Cambridge, and I heard the simple but compelling call of the gospel."

He completed his Cambridge studies, earned his Ph.D. degree from an American university, and then felt called to South Africa. His vision was to conduct citywide evangelistic crusades similar to those of Dr. Graham. What he discovered was a nation whose population was largely nonwhite but whose government was totally dominated by whites, part of the entrenched system of apartheid.

"Apartheid, I was convinced, was evil," Cassidy said. "I knew I had to face the fire of opposing it."

Earlier in his graduate studies in seminary, he had become convinced that the gospel of Christ had a balanced commitment to the saving of souls and the dignity of human life. Spiritual concern could not be separated from social concern. "Justice is love built into structures," Cassidy said. He reminded the audience that John and Charles Wesley had challenged unjust structures and eventually the slavery trade was abolished. "Moral change brought social change," he said.

CONFRONTING APARTHEID

Cassidy decided to tackle apartheid head-on. There were 40 million people in South Africa who called themselves Christians, but most had little interest in applying Christianity to social structures of life.

God's word to the prophet Jeremiah became Cassidy's guiding light. "'For I know the plans I have for you,' declares the LORD, 'plans to prosper you and not to harm you, plans to give you hope and a future. Then you will call upon me and come and pray to me, and I will listen to you. You will seek me and find me when you seek me with all your heart.'"[1] Cassidy said, "These words were spoken to Israel in the darkest hour of Babylonian captivity. God had plans for ancient Israel, and we knew God had plans for us. We are a people of hope, and we knew that God was already at work in South Africa."

The years that followed were difficult. As a leader in the antiapartheid movement, Cassidy was accused by police of working for the CIA. His own nephew refused to fight in the apartheid army and spent six years in prison.

Cassidy's opposition came not only from government leaders but from many white Christians who were satisfied with the status quo. He was convinced that the character of God was total righteousness and that because man is created in God's image, all men have a sense of moral order. He believed that "apartheid was against the grain of the universe. However, the great challenge," he said, " was to come in love." Only God could touch the hearts of people and bring all parties to a peaceful resolution.

So in April 1983 Cassidy called the nation to prayer. He headed a twenty-four-hour prayer chain that focused on praying for the nation. This prayer chain continued for two years; day and night, Christians prayed for God's direction in their nation. All across the nation, people prayed—even on death row, where forty-two inmates were involved in the prayer chain.

LOVE THAT CHALLENGES

Then Cassidy and those who worked with him began to organize weekend retreats, bringing together an equal number of whites and nonwhites. The meetings focused on sharing their autobiographies. Each person shared his own history. One black Christian shared his experience of being put in a pit, covered with dirt, only his head above the soil; then having whites urinate on him. The reality of the atrocities that had taken place began to touch the hearts of whites and nonwhites. And the walls of hostility began to disintegrate. Church leaders began to get involved in the call for justice. The focus was on God and His direction for their nation.

At one juncture, forty million Christians were challenged to stay home from work and invest the day in prayer. That day of prayer brought the nation to a standstill, but it turned the nation's focus on God. When in due time the political leaders agreed to meet and seek to work out a new agreement for the nation's political process, there was much tension. After days of negotiation, it seemed that the whole process would fall apart. At that point, Cassidy and others organized a prayer meeting at a rugby stadium. Over thirty thousand came to pray. While the political leaders met in the stadium box office, the citizens prayed. Later the media would report that "the Jesus peace rally" turned the tide. Peace prevailed, and the nation was allowed free elections that took place in peace.

In Cassidy's words, "We had to face the reality that only God could change the hearts of men and remove apartheid in a peaceful way. It required confessions and repentance, but God intervened in human history. Great things happen on the wheels of relationships."[2]

When love prevails, human social structures can be changed. We can move closer to the ideal of justice, realizing that what Cassidy said is true. "Justice is love built into structures." Only love has the potential of bringing human societies to a higher level of justice, according to Cassidy. However, because of the reality of evil, such love will never be expressed without opposition.

LOVE THAT SACRIFICES

Cassidy described the many atrocities that occurred as South Africa struggled with change. In some of those atrocities, Christian love prevailed at tremendous cost. For example, the Hutu and the Tutsi tribes had been lifelong enemies, but the love of Christ drew members of each tribe into a single church. One Sunday morning as the former enemies worshiped together, the militia encircled the church. They demanded that all members of the Hutu tribe exit from the church building.

The Hutu Christians knew what was about to happen: Their Tutsi brothers were going to be massacred. They could not abandon their Christian brothers, so they refused to exit the building. Once word of their refusal reached the ears of the military leaders, the militia stormed the church. Within moments, all five hundred, Hutu and Tutsi alike, were killed. These Hutu Christians were followers of Jesus who said, "I am the good shepherd. The good shepherd lays down his life for the sheep." Love prevailed!

All of the problems of South Africa have not abated since free elections. Love has not always prevailed, but where there are people who genuinely love God, human relationships will be different. Cassidy was right. "Great things happen on the wheels of relationships." And the oil that lubricates the wheels of relationships is love. No power holds more potential for changing human relationships than the power of love.

LOVE THAT CHANGES PLANS

Love for God may dramatically alter one's plans. Larry Pepper is a teaching physician at Mbarara University Hospital in Uganda. Before January 2, 1996, however, Dr. Pepper was on a totally different vocational track. As a flight surgeon for the National Aeronautics and Space Administration (NASA), he helped in the medical selection of astronauts at the Johnson Space Center in Houston. During actual launches, he shuttled to Florida's Kennedy Space Center, where he headed up emergency medical teams in case of accidents, and then went on to landing sites to assist in crew recovery.

In his seven years with NASA, Dr. Pepper worked in more than fifteen missions, including the first Hubble Space Telescope repair mission. He dreamed of someday making a space flight.

Active in his local church and deeply committed to Jesus Christ, he and his wife, Sally, were raising three children. Now, though, he is more than half a world away in Uganda, Africa, sacrificing his dream and a secure lifestyle. What happened? In the midst of a successful career, Dr. Pepper received a message from God. In his own words, the message was, "'You've committed everything to Me—except your job.'"

"That was the turning point," Pepper says. "I prayed and told God that I wanted Him to put us where He wanted us to be."

Larry and Sally began to pray for God's direction. In a few months, Larry went on a volunteer trip to Zaire, to work with Rwandan refugees. There he met missionary Larry Pumpelly, who told him about the need at Mbarara University Hospital in Uganda. Dr. Pepper knew in his heart this was God's direction.

After his decision to become a missionary, Larry was selected as a finalist for astronaut duty in space. He saw this as a test. Did he really love God more than his former dream?

Love prevailed and since 1996, Larry and Sally have been demonstrating the love of God to patients and interns alike. Among other things, he has instituted an AIDS outpatient clinic.

"We're doing something other AIDS organizations don't do by dealing with the spiritual aspect," Pepper said. He expressed great comfort in knowing that though AIDS patients eventually die, many of them have the assurance of God's love and eternal life before death. He is seeking to demonstrate to the young national physicians whom he trains what it means to be a Christian physician committed to dispensing the love of God along with medical help. Each Thursday night he leads Bible study for interns, focusing on the needs of Ugandan men. Friday evenings, he and Sally offer an alternative to the Mbarara bar scene: "TGIF" ("Thank God It's Friday"). Here medical students have an opportunity to play games, watch movies, and discuss biblical concepts.

On Sunday mornings, the Peppers lead their "church." Sally prepares the prenatal clinic at the hospital for church services and leads children in a Bible study. After Larry checks on his patients, he leads the worship service. On Sunday evenings, together they lead a coed Bible study where they seek to make practical the teachings of Jesus to young Ugandan medical personnel.[3] For this couple, love prevails.

WHEN "LOVERS OF GOD" DO NOT PRACTICE LOVE

Six weeks ago, I made my own journey to Africa. Not Uganda, but the West African country of Benin. I was in the coastal city of Cotonou, sitting in a third-floor room of a small hotel. For the moment, there was no water. The official word from downstairs was, "We have ordered the part. It will be in tomorrow."

I was feeling somewhat frustrated until I turned my thoughts to God. I was reminded almost immediately that if I was feeling helpless and that my life was out of control, perhaps I should reflect upon the hundreds of thousands of black men and women who sailed from these very shores against their will to work on the plantations owned by my an-cestors. I wrote the following words in my journal:

"As I sit here in West Africa and realize the atrocity of slav-ery and how the Christian church in England and America bought into that unholy practice, my heart is saddened. I won-der that the blacks of our generation could ever hear the love of God through white vessels. Only God Himself can help any of us look beyond the rubbish and see the Redeemer."

In every generation, there are those who claim to be "lovers of God," whose behavior belies their profession. They are those who pollute the river of God's love. But every gen-eration also has its John Wesleys, William Wilberforces, Harriet Beecher Stowes, and thousands of others whose names never made the history books. These have been the voices calling out of the darkness to say human exploitation is wrong, what-ever the motive. Christ came to save, never to exploit. "How can you say that you love God whom you have not seen when you do not love your brother whom you have seen?"[4] Jesus made a distinction which has been true throughout human history. There is a difference between profession and posses-sion. Talking the talk is not the same as walking the walk.

Sitting in that third-floor hotel room, I was reminded not only of the atrocities of the past but of the thousands of true followers of Jesus who had come to these same shores of West Africa simply to love. If one were to traverse this huge continent, he would encounter literally thousands of hospitals, clinics, colleges and universities, medical schools, and social service projects started by missionaries who loved God more than an easy life.

West Africa is not called "the graveyard of missionaries" without cause. Among the small group of missionaries with whom I met, one had lost his wife when she was thirty-two.

Almost all had experienced malaria one or more times. Four had been held at gunpoint, gagged, and robbed. Many lived in extremely remote villages inaccessible during the rainy season. But all had a passion for God and a love that could not be stopped by opposition.

These were not explorers whose thrill came from discovering a new waterfall; these were men and women who have experienced the love of God through Jesus Christ our Lord. They were investing their lives in taking that love to others.

And where they go, love always prevails.

THE GOD CONNECTION:
THE MOTIVE AND POWER TO LOVE

Religious Versus Divine Love

To love is to seek the well-being of another. Because man is made in the image of God and God's nature is characterized by love, something in the heart of every person will say yes to love. Love is the right thing to do, we reason. However, people are also estranged from God, and, in our natural state, we tend to love those who love us. "I will seek your well-being as long as you seek my well-being" is the rule of the day. This paradigm of love is the basis for most of the world's religions. Therefore, the love that is expressed by those committed to a religious way of life is typically expressed to those who are within the group.

Jesus was radical. When speaking to one such religious group, He said, "You have heard that it was said, 'Love your neighbor and hate your enemy.' But I tell you: Love your enemies and pray for those who persecute you." The basis of this noble challenge was God Himself. Jesus said, God "causes his sun to rise on the evil and the good, and sends rain on the righteous and the unrighteous. If you love those who love you, what reward will you get? . . . And if you greet only your brothers, what are you doing more than others? Do not even pagans do that?"[5] Jesus clearly distinguished between religiously motivated love and divinely motivated love.

Those who have made the God connection will never be satisfied with merely loving those who love them.

The question is, How do we break free from the gravity of earthly love to experience the freedom of divine love? I am convinced that the answer lies in bringing our weakness to the one who has strength, namely, Jesus of Nazareth.

To a group of religious people who claimed to know God as their Father, Jesus said:

"If God were your father, you would love me, for I came from God and now am here. I have not come on my own; but he sent me. Why is my language not clear to you? Because you are unable to hear what I say. You belong to your father, the devil, and you want to carry out your father's desire. He was a murderer from the beginning, not holding to the truth, for there is no truth in him. When he lies, he speaks his native language, for he is a liar and the father of lies. Yet because I tell you the truth, you do not believe me! Can any of you prove me guilty of sin? If I am telling the truth, why don't you believe me? He who belongs to God hears what God says. The reason you do not hear is that you do not belong to God."[6]

These are extremely harsh words, unless they are true. However, if they are true, they explain why religious people have often been involved in murder and lying. They are simply following the example of their father, the devil. They are sincere people but sincerely wrong.

If Jesus' analysis is true, then the answer to man's dilemma is not to unify the world's religions and bring them together into one great world religion that will institute peace. The world's religions individually or corporately have never led us to experience the kind of divine love of which Jesus spoke. No religion, even the "Christian" religion, has ever produced this kind of love. This kind of love flows only through those who have made the genuine God connection, those who truly follow Christ. Like Christ, they "look to . . . the interests of others"; they "honor one another above [them]selves."[7]

God's Everlasting Love

Saul of Tarsus, who himself was caught up in religion before he made the God connection, put it this way: "Very rarely will anyone die for a righteous man, though for a good man someone might possibly dare to die. But God demonstrates his own love for us in this: While we were still sinners, Christ died for us."[8] Human love might motivate us to die for someone who is good. For example, parents have been known to die so that their children could live. Brothers have donated organs to brothers, but human love does not lift us to the level of dying for our enemies. This love flows only from God and is available to us. Again Paul said, "God has poured out his love into our hearts by the Holy Spirit, whom he has given us."[9]

The Scriptures are clear. God loves us with an everlasting love. He loves us even though we have turned away from Him and walked our own way. Because He is totally righteous and holy, He cannot accept our sinfulness. To do so would violate His justice. The results of our sins puts a chasm between us and God. On the human level, a married couple experiences this gulf when one spouse is unfaithful to the other. The distance is inevitable. Justice demands payment for wrongdoing. Even our own human sense of justice makes such demands. However, since God's love and justice flow equally deep, His love motivated Him to send Jesus, who lived a perfect life and yet endured the full penalty for our wrongdoing. Thus, the demands of justice were met at the cross of Jesus Christ.

Divine Forgiveness Made Possible

On the human scene, Jesus died at the age of thirty-three at the hands of religious people. However, from heaven's perspective, He died as an act of love to pay for the sins of all who would accept God's forgiveness.

Thus He said from the cross moments before He died, "It is finished."[10] He had not come to live a long life or simply to espouse noble teachings. He had come to die, and His purpose was finished. What happened at that moment and three days later have forever changed the lives of those who believe. The historical record is clear.

> *The curtain of the temple was torn in two from top to bottom. The earth shook and the rocks split. The tombs broke open and the bodies of many holy people who had died were raised to life. They came out of the tombs, and after Jesus' resurrection they went into the holy city and appeared to many people. When the centurion and those with him who were guarding Jesus saw the earthquake and all that happened, they were terrified, and exclaimed, "Surely he was the Son of God!"[11]*

What was this curtain that was torn from top to bottom? It was the curtain in the temple that separated the Holy of Holies from the Holy Place. Only the high priest was permitted into the Holy of Holies once a year to offer an animal sacrifice for the sins of the people. All of this was symbolic of Jesus, the Lamb of God, whom the Scriptures say was "slain from the creation of the world."[12] When in the context of time, Jesus, who existed in eternity past with God the Father, invaded human history in the form of a man and became the Lamb slain, temple sacrifices were no longer needed. The symbol had given way to the reality, and all mankind could now be forgiven if they believed. Those holy men and women who had believed God's message and trusted in the death of the sacrificial lamb were raised from the dead. And at the resurrection of Jesus they were taken by Him to the Father to spend eternity in heaven.

The resurrection of Jesus from the dead is the most historically documented event in ancient history. Again and again, those who have examined the evidence of the Resurrection have made the same conclusion: Jesus was raised from the dead three days after He died on a cross. This is the supernatural evidence that the words of Jesus were to be trusted. He was, indeed, God in the flesh, and the words He spoke are true. Those who believe and reach out to accept God's forgiveness receive not only forgiveness but the gift of the Holy Spirit—God's Spirit comes to reside in them, and they now have the love of God to share with their generation. This is what Paul meant when he wrote in Romans 5:5, "God has poured out his love into our hearts by the Holy Spirit, whom he has given us."

SOUNDS INCREDIBLE!

If you are encountering these ideas for the first time, I know that they seem to be incredible. But I know also that because you are made in God's image and because God loves you, there is something within your spirit that says, "Yes, this is truth." It is acting on this response that will bring you to the God connection. The words you say to God are unimportant, but the heart cry is something like this: "Lord, I find it difficult to believe that You love me so much. But I open my heart to You. I want to accept Your forgiveness. I thank You that Christ has paid my penalty. I invite Your Spirit into my life. I want my life to be a channel of Your love. I give myself to You forever."

Thousands of people from cultures around the globe have made that kind of response to God and, in so doing, have found love and life forever. From the lives of these individuals, the love of God is spoken in all five love languages around the world in every generation. One by one, people continue to respond to the love of God and make "the God connection."

LOVE IN BLACK AND WHITE

Unlikely Friends

For over thirty years, one of my closest friends has been Clarence Shuler. From the human perspective, we are unlikely friends. Born in the Deep South before the days of integration, Clarence to black parents and I to white, the chance of our forming a friendship in the late 1960s was not very great. Racial tensions were high; integration of public schools was not being accepted without resistance. The cultural climate did not foster interracial relationships.

I was serving on the staff of an all-white church which had just completed a new gymnasium for its young people. During one "fun night for teens," Clarence and his friend Russell walked into the gymnasium. I could not help but notice them, so I went over, introduced myself, and welcomed them to the evening. They seemed to have a good time and began to attend the meetings regularly.

In our discussion times, Clarence participated freely. He was not afraid to ask questions. He always had a cordial spirit.

When it came time for the youth retreat weekend, Clarence signed up. During that weekend, Clarence would make the God connection. Friday night and Saturday were filled with fun activities. On Saturday night, I gave a lecture and ended with the question, "Is your life complete or is something missing?" In Clarence's own words, he later said, "I had already realized that something was missing in my life. I had thought that if I could make the high school basketball team, all my problems would be solved. Well, after I made the team, I quickly realized that I still had the same problems! I needed Jesus Christ in my life."

Bowing Behind a Pickup Truck

I shall never forget the night that Clarence and I bowed on the ground behind a pickup truck, and he asked Jesus Christ to forgive him of his sins and to come into his life. Clarence says of that experience, "My life really changed! God gave me an inner peace that has stayed with me no matter what the situation. God taught me the freedom of being an individual so that I no longer had to follow the crowd to find acceptance. Most of all, I began to live the wonderful life God had planned for me."

Later Clarence would say, "As excited as I was to have become a Christian, it bothered me that a white man led me to Christ. Later, I realized that to him race didn't matter, and that it shouldn't matter to me. All that mattered was that Christ was now in my life!"

Clarence continued to be active in our youth group and began to study the Scriptures for himself. At that time, Karolyn and I had "open house" for college students every Friday night. He started attending these Friday night meetings regularly. He began to memorize Scripture and share his own faith with others. When summer rolled around, I asked him if he would be willing to serve as a counselor at our church camp. We gave him a group of thirteen-year-old boys, all white. Clarence said, "That's an experience I'll never forget."

Clarence graduated from high school and then completed college and seminary. Since seminary days, Clarence has worked with a variety of Christian organizations. He has served as cross-cultural consultant for churches, colleges, and other Christian institutions. He has authored two books and numerous articles. He is a devoted husband and father.

The Solution to Racial Tensions

Clarence has often publicly and privately expressed appreciation to me for my role in his life. He extols me for my bravery in the late '60s by making him feel welcomed in an all-white church, but I think he was the brave one.

Clarence has taught me much of divine love. He has taught me that love covers a multitude of sins, that love transcends racial boundaries, and that love is always willing to forgive. God was loving me when he brought Clarence Shuler into my life.

I have come to believe that the only solution to the racial tensions of my country and others around the world is divine love. I understand full well that people cannot give what they have not received. The answer is not more sermons on love; the answer is helping people one at a time make the God connection. Once an individual knows God and is controlled by His Spirit, love will flow freely through him.

"LOVE ONE ANOTHER"

Jesus said to those who followed Him while He was on earth, "A new command I give you: Love one another. As I have loved you, so you must love one another. By this all men will know that you are my disciples, if you love one another."[13] Jesus proclaimed that love is the distinguishing mark of those who follow Him. If we are to be God's agents to help others in our generation come to know God in a personal way, it will not be through argumentation or force but through divine love.

Years ago Nicky Cruz, a drug-addicted gang leader on the streets of New York City, confronted David Wilkerson, a young, passionate follower of Jesus.

"You come near me, Preacher, and I'll kill you," Nicky warned.

"You could do that. You could cut me in a thousand pieces and lay them out in the street and every piece would love you," Wilkerson responded.[14]

In time, Nicky became a follower of Jesus. Love prevails.

A LOVE RELATIONSHIP
THAT GOES ON AND ON

We come to God as individuals, but once the God connection is made, He places us into His family. For the rest of our lives and throughout eternity, we are never again alone. We belong to each other.[15] In the family of God, our relationship runs deeper than blood. We are here for the benefit of each other, and together we reach out to those outside the family and become God's agents of love to them.

Receiving Love in All Five Languages

Whatever love language God spoke to draw us to Himself will be the love language we most naturally use to express our love to God. But we must not stop there. We have begun an incredible love relationship with God. It is His desire that we learn to receive His love in all five languages. The apostle Paul expressed it this way:

> *For this reason I kneel before the Father, from whom his whole family in heaven and on earth derives its name. I pray that out of his glorious riches he may strengthen you with power through his Spirit in your inner being, so that Christ may dwell in your hearts through faith. And I pray that you, being rooted and established in love, may have power, together with all the saints, to grasp how wide and long and high and deep is the love of Christ, and to know this love that surpasses knowledge—that you may be filled to the measure of all the fullness of God.*
>
> *Now to him who is able to do immeasurably more than all we ask or imagine, according to his power that is at work within*

us, to him be glory in the church and in Christ Jesus through-out all generations, for ever and ever! Amen.[16]

It is clear: Our relationship with God does not end when we make the God connection. In fact, it just begins. It is also clear that this love relationship with God is in association with other members of the family.

Speaking Love in All Five Languages

Thus as we learn to receive the love of God in all five love languages, we also begin to learn to speak these languages to other members of the family and to those outside the family.

Expressing love using your primary love language will come easy for you. Learning to speak the other four love languages may take time and effort. However, we must remember that we are simply channels of His love. We don't generate the love. Remember, the apostle Paul wrote, "God has poured out his love into our hearts by the Holy Spirit, whom he has given us."

We are not loving others in order to be accepted by God; we are loving others because He has graciously accepted us into His family and loved us. We have responded to His love. Now we are channels of His love to others.

God designed us to live in community with others. Learning to express God's love in all five love languages will enhance our usefulness in the family. When love prevails in the Christian community, the non-Christian world will beat a path to our doors, for they desperately long for such love. Again, hear the words of Jesus: "A new command I give you: Love one another. As I have loved you, so you must love one another. By this all men will know that you are my disciples, if you love one another."

Love is the distinguishing mark of the Christian. When God's love flows through us in all five languages, we become His instruments in helping other individuals make the God connection and enter His family. When this happens, love prevails!

EPILOGUE:
The God Who Speaks Your Language

*T*HIS BOOK IS BEING RELEASED exactly one year after the United States suffered her first attack on native shores. On September 11, 2001, terrorists crashed jetliners into the World Trade Center of New York City and the Pentagon; a fourth jet slammed into the ground as heroic passengers wrestled the hijackers for control of the plane. Almost four thousand American citizens died in New York and Washington, D.C., at the hands of deluded religious zealots. It's another example that man's religions do not hold the key to peace.

The purpose of this book is not to call people to greater religious devotion. The individuals who commandeered the planes that destroyed the Trade Center's Twin Towers and part of the Pentagon had the ultimate in religious devotion. They were willing to sacrifice their own lives for their religious beliefs. But who will argue that their actions were expressions of love?

The religions of the world reveal man's search for the transcendent, but they do not quench the thirst of the human soul. Christianity, when practiced as a religion, is no different. Thousands who call themselves Christians have never made the "God connection." For them, Christianity is their religion—a set of beliefs and certain religious practices, such as attending church, giving money, repeating prayers, and trying to be good citizens. They hope that when they die they will go to heaven, but they have no assurance because they have no relationship with the God of heaven.

They are "cultural Christians." They consider themselves Christian because they grew up in a home where their parents' religion was Christianity.

BEYOND A CULTURAL RELIGION

Such cultural Christians are like cultural Buddhists, Hindus, Jews, or Muslims. They follow the religion of their parents. It is the religion of convenience. They acknowledge their own longings for the transcendent, and their religion provides a vehicle for expressing spiritual hunger—a hunger that is never truly satiated.

Religion often inoculates the individual from making the true "God connection." In this sense, religion becomes a shackle of Satan, restraining people from true spiritual freedom. Refusal to consider a personal response to the love of God because "I have my own religion" is evidence of the tremendous power of religious inoculation.

However, in every generation and in various cultures,

there have been those who have been willing to look beyond their cultural religion in search of the love of God. Their search has been rewarded by the God who said, "You will seek me and find me when you seek for me with all your heart. I will be found by you."

THE GOD WHO REVEALS HIS LOVE

The God who revealed His love to Abraham, Isaac, Jacob, Joseph, Moses, Isaiah, Jeremiah, Ezekiel, and Malachi is the same God who expressed His love supremely by wrapping Himself in human flesh under a Bethlehem star. He is the same God who demonstrated His love to the humble fishermen, Peter, James, and John; a tax collector, Matthew; a physician, Luke; and a religious zealot, Saul of Tarsus. He is the same God who is at work in the world today and continues to express His love to people like those you have met in this book. The good news is He loves you and me as much as anyone else. We are made in His image, and He longs to have a relationship with us.

And He expresses His love to you in your own primary love language:

- To those who understand the love language of words of affirmation, Jesus says, *"Come to me, all you who are weary and burdened, and I will give you rest. Take my yoke upon you and learn from me, for I am gentle and humble in heart, and you will find rest for your souls. For my yoke is easy and my burden is light."*[1]
- To those whose primary love language is gifts, Jesus says, *"My sheep listen to my voice; I know them, and they follow*

me. I give them eternal life, and they shall never perish; no one can snatch them out of my hand."[2]

- To those who desire quality time, the Scriptures say, *"Come near to God and he will come to you."*[3]
- To those whose love language is acts of service, Jesus says of Himself, *"The Son of Man did not come to be served, but to serve, and to give his life as a ransom for many."* When those who knew Him best tried to summarize His life, they simply said, *"He went around doing good and healing all who were under the power of the devil, because God was with him."*[4]
- For those who understand best the love language physical touch, nothing speaks more profoundly than the incarnation of Christ. Here is the way John the apostle described it: *"[What] we have heard . . . seen with our eyes . . . looked at and our hands have touched—this we proclaim."* Indeed, John wrote of Jesus' physical presence: *"We have seen his glory, the glory of the One and Only, who came from the Father, full of grace and truth."*[5] God became man in order to touch us. Follow Him throughout the brief thirty-three years of His earthly journey, and you will find Him touching children, those afflicted with leprosy, the blind, and the deaf. His touch brought healing and hope to all those whom He encountered.

Those of us who live in the twenty-first century do not have the benefit of observing the life and teachings of Jesus, but we do have the record of what He said and did. Jesus clearly claimed that His teachings came from God: "If anyone loves me, he will obey my teaching. My Father will love him, and we will come to him and make our home with him. He who does not love me will not obey my teaching. These words you hear are not my own; they belong to the Father who sent me."[6] Jesus clearly indicated that once He had gone back to God His Father, He would send the Holy Spirit, who would "remind you of everything I have said to you."[7]

God did not leave the writing of the New Testament to man alone but guided the minds of those who were eyewitnesses. John, the apostle who walked with Jesus for three and one-half years, indicated that it would be impossible to record everything that Jesus said and did. But he stated clearly, "These are written that you may believe that Jesus is the Christ, the Son of God and that by believing you may have life in his name."[8]

THE GOD WHO INITIATES LOVE

John also clearly indicated that it was God who initiated love. "We love because he first loved us. If anyone says, 'I love God,' yet hates his brother, he is a liar. For anyone who does not love his brother, whom he has seen, cannot love God, whom he has not seen. And he has given us this command: Whoever loves God must also love his brother."[9]

In this, John was echoing the words of Jesus who, when asked by the religious leaders of His day to point out "the greatest commandment in the Law," answered, "'Love the Lord your God with all your heart and with all your soul and with all your mind.' This is the first and greatest commandment. And the second is like it: 'Love your neighbor as yourself.' All the Law and the Prophets hang on these two commandments."[10]

John summarized it best when he said,

Dear friends, let us love one another, for love comes from God. Everyone who loves has been born of God and knows God. Whoever does not love does not know God, because God is love. This is how God showed his love among us: He sent his one and only Son into the world that we might live through him. This is love: not that we loved God, but that he loved us and sent his Son as an atoning sacrifice for our sins.[11]

Paul, the first-century apostle who did not see Christ in the flesh but who was "touched" by God while he was enroute to persecute those who were followers of Jesus, declared,

The God who made the world and everything in it is the Lord of heaven and earth and does not live in temples built by hands. And he is not served by human hands, as if he needed anything, because he himself gives all men life and breath and everything else. From one man he made every nation of men, that they should inhabit the whole earth; and he determined the times set for them and the exact places where they should live. God did this so that men would seek him and perhaps reach out for him and find him, though he is not far from each one of us. "For in him we live and move and have our being. . . . We are his offspring."

Therefore since we are God's offspring, we should not think that the divine being is like gold or silver or stone—an image made by man's design and skill. In the past God over-looked such ignorance, but now he commands all people every-where to repent. For he has set a day when he will judge the world with justice by the man he has appointed. He has given proof of this to all men by raising [Jesus] from the dead.[12]

THE GOD WHO IS HOLY AND LOVING

In every generation and in every culture, the Spirit of God continues to communicate divine love by speaking the love languages of God. God is both holy and loving. If man does not respond to His love and accept His forgiveness and the gift of an eternal relationship with Him, then man must face His judgment. The fork in the road for all mankind is to choose God's love or God's justice. We either pay for our own wrongdoing or we accept the loving provision of God's payment on our behalf. That payment was made on a rugged cross outside the city of Jerusalem by the Son of God Himself. God's love and justice met on that cross, bringing life and forgiveness to all who believe.

The Cross has become the universal symbol of God's love, for there God spoke all five love languages. From the cross Jesus said, "Father, forgive them, for they do not know what they are doing." What words could speak more deeply of love? In His death, He performed His greatest act of service. By paying the ultimate sacrifice, He reconciled sinful man to the Holy God.[13] The gift He offered was forgiveness of sins and eternal life,[14] which opened the way for man to have an intimate relationship with God by spending quality time with the Creator, both now and forever. On the Cross, God touched man at his point of deepest need and said, "I love you!" Here Jesus fulfilled His promise: "I am the good shepherd. The good shepherd lays down his life for the sheep."

A MESSAGE OF GRACE
AND UNCONDITIONAL LOVE

As an author, I am aware that all I have written in this book about the love of God is but a note in the symphony of God's immeasurable love. The song writer expressed it well:

> *Could we with ink the ocean fill,*
> *And were the skies of parchment made,*

Were every stalk on earth a quill,
And every man a scribe by trade;
To write the love of God above
Would drain the ocean dry;
Nor could the scroll contain the whole,
Tho' stretched from sky to sky.[15]

God has spoken and continues to speak His love in all languages. His message is clear: "I love you even though you have walked away from Me. I desire to forgive you. That is why I have paid for your wrongdoing. I want to have a love relationship with you. If you are willing to turn from your self-seeking path and accept My forgiveness and love, you will be My child forever. I will love you and give you the best possible life both now and for eternity. Open your heart to My love and My spirit, and I will come to live with you."

This is God's desire expressed throughout the Scriptures.

I know the message of God's grace (unmerited favor) and unconditional love seems incredible. By nature, people want to do something to earn God's forgiveness and to make peace with God. The world's religions stand as living monuments to this aspiration. Religious ritual and demands place the emphasis on man's presumed ability to forge his own path to God.

Man can never atone for his own sins. If this were possible, God would have left Adam and Eve wearing fig leaves. Instead, He killed an animal and clothed them with its skin, reminding them that the wages of sin is always death. Because of God's incredible love, He became a man and paid the ultimate penalty for our wrongdoing so that we could be forgiven and live eternally with Him.

⤫

Our part is to simply lift our hands and receive His love. No wonder John the apostle, in describing the nature of God, said simply, "God is love."[16]

We love Him because He first loved us!

NOTES

INTRODUCTION:
THE LOVE CONNECTION

1. *World Book Encyclopedia,* 1970, s.v. "God."

2. Genesis 1:27.

CHAPTER 2:
GOD SPEAKS LOVE LANGUAGE #1: *Words of Affirmation*

1. Jeremiah 31:3 NASB.

2. John 13:1 NASB.

3. 2 Timothy 3:16–17; 2 Peter 1:20–21.

4. Genesis 1:26–27.

5. Hebrews 2:7; cf. Psalm 8:5.

6. Isaiah 48:17–18.

7. Isaiah 41:10; Jeremiah 29:11; 31:3,13.

8. John 5:24; 6:35, 40; 10:27–30; Revelation 22:12–13, 17.

9. Luke 23:34.

10. John 10:9–11.

11. Charles Dudley Warner, ed., vol. 23, *Library of the World's Best Literature* (New York: J.A. Hill & Co., 1896), 9334, 9340.

12. Psalm 119:103–105, 111, 114, 162–165.

13. Psalms 40:16; 69:30–31; 119:97–98; 145:21; 146:1–2.

14. Psalm 119:89, 91–93.

CHAPTER 3:
GOD SPEAKS LOVE LANGUAGE #2: *Quality Time*

1. See Genesis 1–3.

2. Genesis 18:17.

3. Psalm 145:17–18.

4. Isaiah 43:1–2.

5. Psalm 116:1–2.

6. James 4:8.

7. See John 14:23–26.

8. John 17:24; see also 14:16–18.

9. Mark 3:14.

10. George Muller, *Autobiography of George Muller, the Life of Trust* (Grand Rapids: Baker, 1981), 115.

11. Ibid., 89, 101, 108–9.

12. Ibid., 82.

13. Ibid., 138–39.

14. Ibid., 206–7.

15. Ibid., 62.

16. Ibid., 206.

17. See Jonathan Edwards, *The Life and Diary of David Brainerd* (Grand Rapids: Baker, 1989); E. M. Bounds, *Power Through Prayer* (Minneapolis: World Wide Publications, 1989); Charles G. Finney, *The Autobiography of Charles G. Finney* (Minneapolis: Bethany Fellowship, 1977); and Basil Miller, *Praying Hyde: A Man of Prayer* (Grand Rapids: Zondervan, 1943).

18. C. Austin Miles, "In the Garden," verses 1–2 and refrain. In public domain.

CHAPTER 4:
GOD SPEAKS LOVE LANGUAGE #3: *Gifts*

1. R. G. LeTourneau, *Mover of Men and Mountains* (Chicago: Moody, 1972), 143.

2. Ibid., 263.

3. Ibid., 79.

4. Ibid., 204.

5. Ibid., 205.

6. Adapted from LeTourneau, *Mover of Men,* 105.

7. LeTourneau, *Mover of Men,* 278.

8. Ibid., 33.

9. Ibid., 274.

10. Ibid., 275.

11. Ibid., 280.

12. Genesis 1:27, 29–31; emphasis added.

13. Revelation 22:12–14, 16–17.

14. Deuteronomy 7:13.

15. Deuteronomy 11:13–15.

16. 1 Kings 3:7, 9, 11–13.

17. John 3:17, 35–36.

18. John 16:16, 20.

19. John 16:23–24.

20. Ephesians 5:1–2.

21. James 1:17; 1 John 3:1–2.

22. Ephesians 4:11–12.

23. 1 Corinthians 12:7.

24. Matthew 25:34–40.

25. Psalm 19:1–3.

26. Matthew 7:7–11.

27. James 4:3.

CHAPTER 5:
GOD SPEAKS LOVE LANGUAGE #4: *Acts of Service*

1. José Luis Gonzalez-Balado, *Mother Teresa: In My Own Words* (Ligouri, Mo.: Liguori, 1996), ix.

2. Ibid., x.

3. Ibid., 24, 26, 30.

4. Ibid., 34.

5. Ibid., 33.

6. Ibid., 38, 80.

7. Ibid., 107.

8. Ibid., 108–9.

9. Romans 15:6; see also 2 Corinthians 1:3 and Ephesians 1:3.

10. Psalm 115:4–7, 9, 12–13.

11. Luke 4:18–19; Jesus' quotation of Isaiah 61:1–2.

12. Luke 4:21, 24.

13. John 17:1–5.

14. John 14:1–7.

15. John 14:8–11.

16. John 15:24–25.

17. Jesus rose to life a widow's son, a ruler's daughter, and an older man and friend who had been in the grave four days. These miracles are recorded in Luke 7:11–17; 8:41–42, 49–56; and John 11:1–44, respectively.

18. John 15:9.

19. John 15:12–13; Luke 23:34.

20. Romans 5:6–8.

21. John 17:24, 26.

CHAPTER 6:
GOD SPEAKS LOVE LANGUAGE #5: *Physical Touch*

1. Psalms 68:5; 27:10.

2. Genesis 32:25, 30, 31.

3. Exodus 34:29, 33.

4. Mark 10:13.

5. Mark 10:15–16.

6. John 9:11.

7. Matthew 8:2–3, 15.

8. Matthew 9:27, 29–30.

9. Matthew 17:2–3, 5–8; see also Mark 9:2–10 and Luke 9:28–36.

10. John 13:1–4.

11. John 13:12-15, 17.

12. José Luis Gonzalez-Balado, *Mother Teresa: In My Own Words* (Ligouri, Mo.: Liguori, 1996), 35.

13. Acts 3:6–10.

14. Acts 3:12–13, 16.

15. Acts 3:18–21.

16. Acts 9:4–9.

17. Acts 9:17–19.

18. Acts 9:20–22.

CHAPTER 8:
LEARNING TO SPEAK NEW DIALECTS OF LOVE

1. See, for example, Romans 1:21.

2. Robert J. Morgan, *From This Verse* (Nashville: Nelson, 1998), 362.

3. Psalm 42:1–2.

4. Matthew 10:42.

5. John 20:30–31.

6. Acts:10:38.

7. I learned Lisa's story from my friend Joe Stowell, president of Moody Bible Institute.

8. Luke 7:38.

CHAPTER 9:
WHEN LOVE SEEMS DISTANT

1. For further information on the relationship between love languages and discipline, see Ross Campbell and Gary Chapman, *The Five Love Languages of Children* (Chicago: Northfield, 1997), 117, 124–27.

2. Hebrews 12:5–7, 10–11.

3. R. G. LeTourneau, *Mover of Men and Mountains* (Chicago: Moody, 1972), 85.

4. Psalm 42:1–2.

5. 2 Corinthians 12:9–10.

6. 2 Timothy 4:6–7.

7. John 10:11, 17–18.

8. John 11:25.

CHAPTER 10:
WHEN LOVE PREVAILS

1. Jeremiah 29:11–13.

2. Michael Cassidy, "Loose in the South African Fire," C. S. Lewis Foundation Summer Institute (Oxbridge '98), 24 July 1998; author's personal notes.

3. Heidi Soderstrom, "Prescription: Hope," *The Commission,* May 1999, 34–37.

4. 1 John 4:20 (author paraphrase).

5. Matthew 5:43–47.

6. John 8:42–47.

7. Philippians 2:4; Romans 12:10.

8. Romans 5:7–8.

9. Romans 5:5.

10. John 19:30.

11. Matthew 27:51–54.

12. Revelation 13:8.

13. John 13:34–35.

14. David Wilkerson with John and Elizabeth Sherrill, *The Cross and the Switchblade* (New York: Random House, 1963), 72.

15. See Psalm 68:6; Romans 12:5; Ephesians 3:15.

16. Ephesians 3:14–21.

EPILOGUE:
THE GOD WHO SPEAKS YOUR LANGUAGE

1. Matthew 11:28–30.

2. John 10:27–28.

3. James 4:8.

4. Matthew 20:28; Acts 10:38.

5. 1 John 1:1; John 1:14.

6. John 14:23–24.

7. John 14:26.

8. John 20:31; see also John 21:25.

9. 1 John 4:19–21.

10. Matthew 22:36–40.

11. 1 John 4:7–10.

12. Acts 17:24–31.

13. See Colossians 1:20–22.

14. See John 3:16–18; 1 John 1:9.

15. Frederick M. Lehman, "The Love of God." In public domain.

16. 1 John 4:8, 16.

Delve deeper into the love languages of God through an interactive study of the bestselling book!

LifeWay Christian Resources has created *The Love Languages of God*, an eight session interactive study that brings out greater insights—through daily, individual study and weekly small group interaction. Equip your small groups to discover the depths of God's love languages.

Leader Kit 0-6330-9673-3
Member Book 0-6330-9672-5
Member Book, Spanish Edition 1-4158-2289-1

To purchase, call 800.458.2772, order online at www.lifeway.com, or visit the LifeWay Christian Store serving you.

THE FIVE LOVE LANGUAGES

We all want to love and be loved. But how can we learn to express that love—especially to our mate? By learning his or her "love language," says Dr. Gary Chapman. It's a message that's positive, hopeful, and easy to apply—as millions of readers have already discovered.
ISBN 1-881273-15-6
Audio CD Version ISBN 1-881273-37-7
Oasis Audio Unabridged Version ISBN 1-58926-906-3

THE FIVE LOVE LANGUAGES JOURNAL

Now you can journal your thoughts, feelings, and progress on keeping your mate's love tank full with *The Five Love Languages Journal.* Use the entries to spark communication, or keep them as a private retreat. Duotone faux-leather will appeal to both men and women.
ISBN 1-881273-71-7

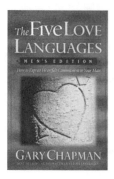

THE FIVE LOVE LANGUAGES MEN'S EDITION

Men, how can you learn to speak (and understand) the love language of the woman in your life? This special edition of the bestselling *The Five Love Languages* includes new features just for men! Complete the profile and discover her—and your—love language; then try out some of the new end-of-chapter ideas on showing heartfelt love to that special woman in your life.
ISBN 1-881273-10-5
Oasis Audio Unabridged Version ISBN 1-59859-066-9

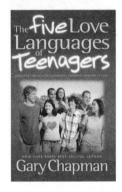
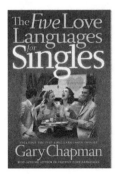

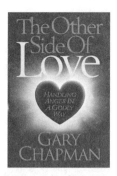

THE OTHER SIDE OF LOVE

Many of us need help with anger. But can anger be used for good? Yes, says Dr. Gary Chapman, who shows us how we can move anger "from one side to another"—toward love.

ISBN 0-8024-6777-6

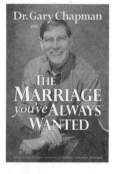

DR. GARY CHAPMAN ON THE MARRIAGE YOU'VE ALWAYS WANTED

Take a fresh look at marriage through the lens of Dr. Gary Chapman, as he draws on years of counseling experience. He offers practical, faith-based wisdom on how to communicate, rekindle love, avoid financial bondage, and more.

ISBN 0-8024-8786-6

Oasis Audio Unabridged Version ISBN 1-59859-008-1

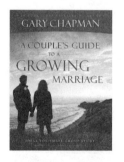

A COUPLE'S GUIDE TO A GROWING MARRIAGE

Marriage is meant to be the most intimate of human relationships, but for many couples this intimacy is only a dream. This book will help you make that dream a reality. So much more than a personal and group study, it will teach you to share your life more fully with God, and as this relationship deepens, so will your relationship as a couple.

ISBN 0-8024-7299-0

THE FIVE LANGUAGES OF APOLOGY

Just as you have a different love language, you also hear and express the words and gestures of apology in a different language. Gary Chapman has teamed with counselor Jennifer Thomas on this groundbreaking study of the way we apologize, discovering that it's not just a matter of will— it's a matter of how.

ISBN 1-881273-57-1

Oasis Audio Unabridged Version ISBN 1-59859-149-5

PARENTING YOUR ADULT CHILD

Few resources are available to help parents communicate with their child who is no longer a child. Here's a tool that will help you deal with such issues as: Helping Your Child Find Success, When Adult Children Return with their Children, and more.

ISBN 1-881273-12-1

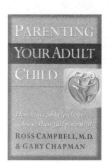

FIVE SIGNS OF A LOVING FAMILY

In modern Western culture, it is widely acknowledged that the family is in serious trouble. Despite the odds, you desire to have family relationships that are fully loving and functional. If you want to establish healthy patterns in your own family, you'll need to learn how to recognize and apply the qualities they share.

ISBN 1-881273-92-X

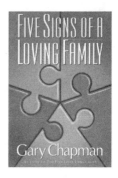

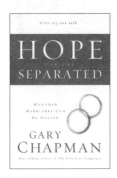